MY LIFE WITH

LUTHER

MY LIFE WITH

LUTHER

A Glimpse of a Legendary American Broadcaster

JAMES HOWARD / HOLLY ABERNATHY

Manufactured in the United States of America
2013 – First Edition

For information regarding special discounts for bulk purchases, please contact:
info@6qCreative.com.

ISBN: 061576519X
ISBN 13: 9780615765198
Library of Congress Control Number: 2012918633
6qCreative Press,
Nashville, TN

Dedication

To my wife, Christy, who also grew up listening to Luther every morning, hoping to hear him say, "No school today due to snow."

To my girls, Gracie and Lucy, who will always be Daddy's little girls no matter how old they are.

To all the Chattanooga residents who have allowed Luther to be part of their lives every morning, year after year. – J.D.H

To my husband, Matt. Thank you for always listening and supporting the next project. This would not have been possible without you.

To my children, Shannon and Iain. Seeing the world through your eyes is my greatest privilege, and it is my heart's desire that, even as you age, you will always have the courage to pursue your dreams. – H.M.A.

Luther in his early days of radio.

Table of Contents

Foreword

There are countless stories of the lives that have been touched by Luther Masingill, far too many to be captured in these pages. Chances are, if you've picked up this book, you have your own story to tell about the role Luther played in your life.

Like so many Chattanoogans, I grew up listening to Luther. We all know that Luther's impact goes far beyond stories of young children being reunited with a family pet or announcements of community events. He has been there with us as we celebrated milestones and through our most trying times as a community and nation. He reported on the bombing of Pearl Harbor as many of our parents and grandparents listened. And, much too recently, on September 11, 2001, he reported to so many of us as we went about our morning routines that our country was under attack.

Luther is a part of Chattanooga — its people, its history and its transformation. He stood by this city from a time when we were one of the most polluted cities in the country to our years of revitalization and transformation. He inspires us with his love of the city and the people who live here. Despite offers from other larger, more attractive markets, he never left the city he loves. Luther has served our community for over 70 years as a broadcaster and so much more.

Thank you, Luther, for your lifetime of service and friendship to our great city.

U.S. Senator Bob Corker

Introduction

James Howard is the co-host of Chattanooga's Sunny 92.3 WDEF-FM radio morning show. Every morning James shares the airwaves with his longtime childhood hero, Luther Masingill. I have worked with James for many years and have watched him evolve from a young student in college to a professional, experienced broadcaster. I have worked with both Luther and James for many years at WDEF-FM and have had the privilege of watching them interact and their friendship grow. Because of this history, I know what an honor it is for James to work alongside Luther everyday. I understand the role Luther has played in James' life. When James came to me for help on this project, I was equally excited about the concept. I was privileged to accept the challenge of turning his idea into a story. I was honored to write and piece together this project and to give Chattanooga and the world a view into the life of broadcasting legend, Luther Masingill. While James wanted to tell Luther's story, I felt it was also important to find a way to interweave the lives of these two men while telling that story. It is, after all, James' account of his life with Luther. Three years later, after numerous interviews and countless hours of research, *My Life with Luther: A Glimpse of a Legendary American Broadcaster* was born.

In these pages you will get a revealing look into the lives of both broadcasters. The story of Luther will unfold through the eyes of James. Interspersed with James' narration are Luther's own words, set off by italics, gleaned from hours of recorded interviews that James conducted with Luther. It is an intimate, yet historical look into the life and times of both men. Of these men, Luther is a legendary broadcaster and James is walking closely in his footsteps. But what is a broadcaster? We all know the meaning of the word – someone who broadcasts on radio or television and delivers information to us. But what does broadcaster mean? What does a broadcaster really do? They do more than broadcast on radio or television and provide us with information. They become a part of our lives, and if they stay in one place long enough, in a way they become part of our family. We get to know them and we learn to trust them. We turn to them and trust them as a reliable source of information. For some, it may seem difficult to fathom the idea that there are hundreds, thousands, or even millions hearing the voice or seeing the face of just one broadcaster.

Most young broadcasters would define that as success. They seek bigger audiences in larger markets – thousands, even millions of listeners and viewers – while consequently achieving status and acquiring more money. Nowadays, young broadcasters getting started in the industry come and go, gaining valuable experience and then move on to bigger cities. It is rare that you find one that stays with his community simply because he cares and he wants to be there. Rarely do you find someone that actually turns down offers to go to larger markets, and with it, turns down more notoriety and more money. Rarely do you find someone that turns down those opportunities and chooses to stay exactly where he is for 72 years. Rarely, in this case, means never. Never in the history of broadcasting has there been a broadcaster who has remained with the same station in the same time slot longer than Luther Masingill.

Interestingly, Luther never dreamed of becoming a broadcaster. It just "kind of happened," if that's the way you believe life works. Regardless of luck or serendipity, what we have here is a seemingly ordinary life that has, over time, turned into something extraordinary. Within the pages of this book, we hope to introduce you to this legendary broadcaster and to give you a glimpse into this extraordinary life and career. This work is not meant to be a comprehensive biography of Luther's life, but rather a way to share an overview of his story from a unique perspective, James' perspective. It is a way to express who Luther is and explain his contributions to the world of communications and broadcasting. Our desire is to convey a glimpse of his life from the mind and experiences of his successor, as well as from Luther's very own words. We desire to give you a more complete picture of the man that you may have heard on the radio and seen on television for so many years, but yet know so little about. For those who do not know Luther, we hope to highlight the ways a broadcaster can truly have an impact on the lives of others and in the community in which they serve. We want to introduce you to Luther, who he really is and how he became a legend in broadcasting. In the process, it is our sincere hope that you are inspired as we take this journey and are able to find a little bit of yourself in *My Life with Luther*.

Holly Abernathy,
Co-Author

MY LIFE WITH

LUTHER

1

A Childhood Hero

On-Air. The red light above the studio entrance was on, indicating those inside were live on the air. I peered through the small soundproof glass window and got a glimpse of my childhood hero as he was sitting in the WDEF Radio booth. This was the voice I had heard growing up, and the voice of the man that inspired me to pursue a career in broadcasting. This was the man, the broadcaster, that had made such an impact on my life as he spoke to thousands, and yet to one. He was speaking to me and to my family at the breakfast table in the mornings before school, to my dad on his commute to work, and to countless other people in similar ways for decades. I was finally looking at the man that I still to this day consider one of the greatest influences in my life, Luther. Yes, just Luther, as he is known here in Chattanooga and the Tennessee Valley. His name is Luther Masingill, the man with an unprecedented history as a radio broadcaster for more than seventy years with the same station, and television broadcaster since the very first broadcast of WDEF Television. Luther Masingill, radio and TV legend, household name and the most familiar voice and face in media here in my hometown of Chattanooga, Tennessee.

Photo courtesy of James Howard

James with his dog Andy, Christmas 1985.

My first experience with Luther was when I lost my dog Andy. I was somewhere around nine or ten years old, and I will never forget coming downstairs on that perfect Christmas morning. The fireplace was lit and toys and gifts surrounded the tree while Christmas music was playing softly in the background on WDEF Radio. With my mom and dad having four children, I knew we were all very fortunate to have gifts to open on Christmas. This particular Christmas was even more special than others had been in the past. Santa Claus, as I innocently believed then, brought me a dog. He was a cocker spaniel and he was named Andy. He was *my* Andy. I fed him morning, noon, and night. I played with him every moment I was home.

Andy became my best friend, but I woke up one morning and Andy was not there. He was gone and I was absolutely devastated. Even after several days, my family continued to search for him, driving all over the neighborhood in the mornings before I had to catch the bus for school. One morning, we spent so much time looking for him that I missed the bus. My sisters and I piled back into my mom's big brown station wagon. As we pulled up into the circular driveway at East Brainerd Elementary School, I remember feeling so worried about Andy. I was just a young boy who was used to the companionship of his dog and to feeding him and taking care of him. That morning, I stood there with my backpack as both of my sisters got out of the car and went up the stairs into the school. My mom tenderly reached for me and said, "James, when I get home, I'm going to call Luther and I'm going to make sure he puts it on the radio. He will find Andy." Saying goodbye to my mother that morning, I proceeded up those long stairs in front of the school. Walking down the hallway toward my first class, I felt a sense of peace and confidence because I believed that Luther was going to find my dog.

In our house, listening to Luther on the radio around the breakfast table was a tradition. Whether we were eating toast, eggs, or cereal, every morning Luther was there. While the breakfast may have changed, Luther did not. He was a constant in our family and we never questioned the presence of his voice on the radio in our home. One morning shortly after losing my dog Andy, we were sitting around the breakfast table and the phone rang. My mom picked up the phone. "Shh! Shh! It's Luther! Hi Luther. You did? Okay, let me grab a pen and jot down the number. Thank you so much Luther!" I remember sitting there and hearing mom's voice as she spoke to Luther on the telephone. At that moment, I knew everything was going to be okay. Sure enough, Andy was found about a mile from our house and I'll never forget the sound of the chain link fence as I opened it to get him. I was so thrilled to get my dog back, thanks to Luther. From that moment on, I was in awe of the fact that he found him. Luther moved from the airwaves of the radio and into my life the day he found Andy.

As a child growing up, my granddad would occasionally pick me up from school. In our conversations he would say, "Yeah, I heard Luther mention...". Later, we would be at the grocery store and you would hear someone else say, "Luther was talking about that on the radio this morning." As I grew up, these memories were stored in my mind and I began to wonder what it would be like to be on the radio just like Luther. "I wonder what he's really like," I thought. After years of listening to WDEF Radio and after finding my dog Andy, Luther was very quickly becoming my childhood hero.

Growing up listening to WDEF Radio, I knew that Luther had a guy who reported the traffic conditions for him. His name was Commander Dean Tobler. Listening to Commander Dean Tobler give the traffic reports from an airplane excited me. I have always loved airplanes and anything to do with flight.

James taking flight lessons in 1986.

Just knowing that he was reporting traffic for Luther from an airplane thrilled me. I remember thinking what an incredible opportunity it would be to report traffic for Luther. I began to think about being a traffic reporter on the radio. When I was about 12 or 13 years old, I mentioned this to my dad. "Dad, the traffic reporter, do you think he lives here in Chattanooga?" I inquired. "Yeah, yeah. He does traffic for Luther," he said. "Dad, that would be such a cool job to fly over Chattanooga and report traffic," I told him. "He's up in the airplane talking to Luther, and he is helping people get to work every day. I want to be that person." My dad looked at me and said, "Let's write him a letter. You write it and I'll make sure it gets to him." Later, my dad went upstairs and found Commander Dean Tobler's address. I feel a bit silly looking back on it now, but I wrote him a letter. I will never forget that day and thinking, "Wow, Commander Dean and Luther, what a cool gig that would be!"

The only radio I ever knew was Luther radio, WDEF Radio. That is what we listened to and all I really knew. Of course as a child, I had aspirations of being on the radio, but when it came time to actually choose a career and obtain some direction, I found myself unprepared. In 1990, I was a junior in high school. The school was holding a career day, and I had thirty minutes in between classes to walk into the cafeteria and scan some options. My life changed that day when, in the sun-washed cafeteria, light was reflecting on a sign that said, "Welcome To Career Day at Tyner High School, Broadcasting Radio and Television." Underneath that sign at a booth was a face that has long been recognized in Chattanooga media, David Carroll from WRCB-TV Channel 3. I walked up to David, shook his hand, and said, "I can sort of see this, me getting into radio. How do you do it?" David Carroll proceeded to give me some advice: "Go to your favorite radio station and work for free."

Work for free is exactly what I did at a new Christian radio station in town, RX-107. I was a fan of Christian music and was involved with my youth group at church. Soon after David Carroll recommended that I begin my career in broadcasting by working for free, I met my first radio boss, Alan Knowles. Alan was the general manager of RX-107 and the station was sponsoring a concert at our church. Before the concert, I walked up to him and said, "I would like to get into radio." He replied by telling me to stop by his office sometime that week. Alan will tell you to this day that when I walked into his office that same week he thought, "This guy is for real." So many times people would come up to him after a performance or during a live remote broadcast and express interest in a career in radio broadcasting. Time and time again he would say, "Well, if you're really serious about it, come by the station and fill out an application and then we'll talk." Nine times out of ten, they wouldn't do it. When I walked into his office and told him, "I can start today," he knew I was serious. He looked at me and said, "You know, afternoons can get kind of hectic. It would be

Photo courtesy of James Howard

James in the studio of his first radio job at RX-107.

nice, when traffic comes down, for you to record traffic, put it on a cart and give it to the announcer." So that day I recorded traffic, and as fate would have it, the traffic reporter was none other than Commander Dean Tobler. He was flying over Chattanooga and reporting traffic conditions: "Here we go. Standby stations in 3, 2, 1.... Here's what traffic looks like over the 75/24 split...." I recorded that, put it on reel-to-reel, and then put it on a cart to deliver to the announcer so he could put it on the air. Alan took me into the studio. A guy whose on-air name was Justin Case was doing afternoons. He said, "You want to push this button? You want to hit the next song?" Being just a kid in high school, I stood there trembling. I was so nervous that my finger was shaking as I reached to hit the button that would play the next song. I was about to start the music that thousands of people were going to hear. I was exhilarated by the experience and it was only the beginning. I worked six months for absolutely no pay.

My mom would give me a hard time, saying, "James, I think they are just using and abusing you." I know my mom was just looking out for me, but I don't think she saw the potential at the time. Regardless of her opinion, she was very supportive of my endeavors as I chose to pursue a career in broadcasting. Finally, a paid position came open at RX-107. I was the first one in line, declaring, "I earned this spot to be paid with this radio station." I got the job and I'm still doing traffic on the radio today. Years after writing the letter to Commander Dean Tobler, I had the pleasure of meeting him personally, but it all started with Luther. I aspired to be like Commander Dean Tobler because he was Luther's traffic reporter.

RX-107 was soon scheduled to go off the air for good and I still didn't have a firm direction in my life. When RX-107 went off the air in 1993, I thought for sure that was the end of my career in radio. Radio veteran Bobby Daniels powered down the transmitter and the entire air staff was in the studio saying goodbye. We played our favorite songs and were sharing with the listening audience what RX-107 had meant to us over the years. After saying goodbye and the transmitter was powered down, I thought my career in broadcasting was over. Having graduated high school and now with RX-107 off the air, I was not sure what was next in my life. I had made a commitment to be a camp counselor during the summer, but that's all that was going on at the time. Two days before I was supposed to leave for six weeks of camp, I received a phone call from my friend and former RX-107 co-worker, Bobby Daniels. Bobby told me they were starting up a CCM (Contemporary Christian Music) Sunday show on 102.7, much like the CCM Sunday currently on Sunny 92.3. At that moment I had to stop and really think about it. Was I supposed to be in broadcasting? Was this what I wanted to do with my life? I made a tough phone call to the camp administrators and explained, "I have this opportunity in radio and I am going to take it."

I started the CCM Sunday job four or five weeks after RX-107 went off the air. That fall I also began attending Chattanooga State Technical Community College. I was doing the CCM Sunday show and attending Chattanooga State when one of my professors, Skip Hill, approached me. He had heard some of my airchecks and projects and he asked, "James, would you be interested in an internship at WDEF-TV?" There I was, an 18-year-old kid wondering what I was going to do with my life. I had some free time during the week since I was doing the CCM Show on Sundays, so I told him I was interested. Skip set up an interview with the production manager at the time, Bill Carter. I met with Bill and he said, "We are looking for a camera operator and we need you to start Monday. Are you interested?" I had some free time so I told him, "Sure!" It ended up not even being an internship, but a full-time job. I was doing mornings, the noon show, and audio on WDEF-TV beginning every weekday at 3:30 in the morning. Shortly after I began working at WDEF Television, Skyler McKenzie (the on-air name used by WDEF Radio operations manager, Danny Howard) heard about my experience in radio and asked me if I wanted to work part-time for Sunny 92.3 WDEF Radio. Of course I said yes and I suddenly found myself working a full-time job in television, working part-time at Sunny 92.3, hosting the CCM show on Sundays, and attending Chattanooga State. As I look back, I realize that was the busiest time in my life, but it was also one of the most exciting times too.

Back when I took that first radio job at RX-107, I could not have known the road I was about to travel. I knew it was going to be a challenging road, but I also knew it was going to be an exciting one. Ever since I heard Luther's voice on the radio as a child and saw how he was able to help people and make a difference in the community, I knew I wanted to become a broadcaster. Before I began to work part-time at Sunny 92.3 WDEF Radio, I was already in the WDEF building as an employee in television. Back then, the WDEF News 12 television studios were on the bottom floor of a building on South Broad Street, the section now known as Luther Masingill Parkway. The WDEF Radio studios were upstairs in the same building (only later having moved to another location down on South Broad Street). My first day on the job at WDEF Television, I did not know I was about to meet my childhood hero, the man that had inspired me to take this path in broadcasting. Still dark at 3:30 a.m., a man who is still a very dear friend of mine, Lee Hope, met me at the door of the station. Lee, now a television director for CBS Chicago, is about the same age as me and was just getting his start in broadcasting as well. He met me at the door to the studios on South Broad Street and gave me the grand tour of the WDEF News 12 studios.

When the tour ended, Lee said, "Hey, let's go up and meet Luther." Luther had already begun his morning radio show, and as we proceeded to go upstairs to the radio studios, I could hear Luther's voice over the hallway speakers. The only time I had ever seen Luther was on television on News 12 when I was sick and had stayed home from school. I ate tomato soup and grilled cheese sandwiches while watching Luther on the noon show after he had finished his radio shift. I remember calling out, "That's what Luther looks like!" As Lee and I walked up the stairs that early morning, he said we needed to be quiet because the on-air light was red, indicating that Luther was live on the radio. As we approached the studios, I looked through the small square window on the door. In that studio, a sort of magic existed during those pre-dawn moments. The sun had not yet begun to rise and the twilight sky seemed to gently reflect off the enormous soundproof, glass windows. Those windows framed the real-life work of art that is Lookout Mountain, as displayed for the announcer who was fortunate enough to be on duty at that unspoiled hour. There was something enchanting about that time of the morning, knowing it was before most people in the city were awake. It felt as if you were some sort of informational caretaker with unparalleled responsibility, a voice for the city. You were alone in the control room, watching the sun nudge one of the city's mountainous jewels from its slumber, along with the rest of the listeners within the sound of your voice. Within that closed, sound-proofed space, it seemed as though the world was perfect, even if only for a moment. I will never forget, as Lee and I stood there, the amazement I felt at watching my childhood hero do what he has done all these years. I was finally seeing what I had only ever *heard* as a child. There was Luther talking into the microphone.

For many years I had listened to him through that very same microphone, his voice coming from the speaker of our little kitchen radio. There I was that morning, standing within five feet of him as he talked live to thousands of people as they awoke and began to prepare for the day.

Photo by Daisy Moffatt

Luther on the air, just as he has been for so many years, September 2012.

The morning I met Luther for the first time at the WDEF Radio studios was a pivotal moment for me. I had worked in radio before and was just getting my start in television broadcasting, but that day was truly a decision-making moment in my life. The experience I had that morning after seeing Luther in the WDEF studios for the first time changed the direction of my life. I was able to see how being a broadcaster made a difference in someone else's life. Luther had made such an impact on me and I wanted to do the same for others and for the city of Chattanooga. Luther and WDEF Radio represented the tradition and history of the city. People have always trusted Luther and displayed confidence in WDEF.

Luther (upper left) featured in early WDEF promotional material reading news scripts as a young man.

It has often been called "Luther's station." WDEF has been around for a long time and is a station with history, a station with a narrative in the community.

I told the station management at the time, general manager Gary Downs and program director Danny Howard, that I was just honored to be a part of the tradition of WDEF. I wanted to express to them how important that was to me as I was being considered for full-time employment. The opportunity to be part of an organization like WDEF was one I did not want to slip away. The morning I met Luther and toured the WDEF studios was definitely a pivotal moment regarding the direction of my life and my career.

Just as the WDEF tradition has contributed to building the community of Chattanooga, I knew an organization like WDEF had been built upon the personal strengths of its leaders. I have always been the type of guy to try to recognize these traits and I saw them in Luther, as well as in my own family. I watched my dad and my granddad as they both served their country in the military, and I never saw anyone work harder at their jobs. I had heard about Luther's military service as well. These men were all role models for me as I observed them working the same jobs for many, many years. They were consistent. As I was growing up, I often associated the characteristics I viewed in my dad and grandfather with Luther. I observed him to be as stable as my granddad and my dad, and I always associated him with strong, patriotic, godly men. Even before I met Luther, I think I placed him on that pedestal. I viewed him as having the same desirable characteristics as my dad and granddad, the kind of characteristics that a young man can look at and aspire to achieve when he grows up. Like them, I too wanted to serve in the military. My entire life I was aware that I was a member of a military family. My dad, my granddad, my uncles, my ancestors, they all either fought in a war or somehow, some way, served their country in the military. Later in life, I had the opportunity to be a part of the aviation program of the Coast Guard Auxiliary, and even though it is a volunteer organization, it allowed me to identify with my family and with Luther. I have always looked up to Luther because he did his part with the military too, having fought in World War II. He served his country and he is one of the hardest working people I know, having been with the same radio station for over 70 years. The stability I saw in Luther is one of the many things that I continue to admire in him. My dad, my granddad, and Luther all set a standard for me, and at some point in my life, I looked at them and knew that whatever I chose to do with my life, that was the way I needed to do it. I wanted to strive for the characteristics I saw modeled in these men.

After that day of seeing Luther in his studio for the first time and eventually gaining the privilege of working alongside of him daily, he continued to have an impact on my life. Whether it was career or marriage and family advice, he has always been there for me. Luther came into my life personally at the age of 19, but I had listened to him all my life on the radio. Hearing him on the air made me feel like I was right there with him. A talented broadcaster can provide that experience for the listener and Luther accomplishes that. He makes you feel like he is talking directly to you.

That first day when I met Luther was the day I decided I wanted a career in broadcasting. I knew for sure that being on the radio was exactly what I wanted to do. I pictured a career in radio and television, while imagining the red on-air lights, ripping news scripts and the smell of fresh-brewed coffee. I imagined the sun rising and people all across the city beginning to arise with it, knowing that those same people were about to tune in to hear news and issues being talked about on the air for the first time. I had an opportunity to be part of an industry that I loved, and I knew that it would be a privilege and an honor to do it. So when my childhood hero moved beyond my ears and my kitchen table to being a physical presence in my daily life at the WDEF broadcast studios, I knew that I wanted to follow in his footsteps. I wanted to be a broadcaster that had an impact on one person and, at the same time, on thousands. Luther went from my companion as a child riding to school every morning to the same companion as I commuted to work every day as an adult. Luther Masingill is a radio and television legend and one of the greatest influences in my life. He is a man with an unprecedented history as a radio broadcaster for more than 70 years with the same station, and a television broadcaster with WDEF-TV since its inception. His is the most familiar name and voice in the Tennessee Valley. He is Luther Masingill, otherwise known as Luther.

Photo by Daisy Moffatt

Luther

2

Luther's Early Years

William Luther Masingill was born on March 9, 1922, to William Tom and Mary Masingill in Chattanooga, Tennessee. During one of the many interviews with Luther for this book, I asked him what hospital he was born in and he started laughing, looking at me like I was crazy. He jokingly said they did not have hospitals back then and that he was born at home.

I was born at home. My doctor's name was Boone. Boone was a famous name back then. His name was Dr. Luther Boone. In fact, Daddy used to joke about how he had eight children and Dr. Boone brought them all into the world. He said he couldn't afford to pay him because there were so many of us, so he named me Luther, after Dr. Luther Boone, the doctor who brought me into this world. I came along about the middle of the eight. There were five boys and three girls in the family. They're all gone except three of us now. It was a big family.

My dad was William Tom Masingill. He was a Chattanoogan and I think he was born out in the Harrison, Tennessee, area. He married a woman from Kentucky named Mary Harlow. He was a big cut-up and he loved to joke and kid around. I am a lot like him in that way. My dad was what they called a "drummer." He drove around and took orders for a wholesale house, and sometimes I'd go with him during the summer when school was out.

From the personal collection of Luther and Mary Masingill

Young Luther (middle) with his siblings in the mid 1920s.

From the personal collection of Luther and Mary Masingill

Luther (back row, seventh from left) with his fifth-grade class from Avondale Grammar School in Chattanooga, Tennessee, in 1933.

From the personal collection of Luther and Mary Masingill

All the male members of the Masingill family in 1941: (back row, left to right) Luther, Tom, David, Mr. Masingill, (front row) Charlie and JT.

One day we were in a small community out near Harrison and Daddy was inside the local store taking orders for candy and chewing gum. As I sat there on that hot summer day waiting for him in his Model T Ford, he came to the screen door. I can still remember how it had "Buy Colonial Bread" embedded in the screen wire. That's the way they used to do it back in those days. "You want something cold to drink, Son?" he asked. He brought me out a good cold bottle of Nehi Grape soda. I'll always remember that. That was how I was introduced to Nehi Grape. That was my first one and I've liked them ever since.

I'll never forget the smell of Juicy Fruit as well. To this day whenever I smell Juicy Fruit Gum, I think of my days riding around with Daddy because he took a couple of boxes with him so he wouldn't have to have them sent out. Many people ordered chewing gum at the time and a lot of it was Juicy Fruit. To this day I still associate the smell of Juicy Fruit Gum with Daddy and riding around with him on his route around Chattanooga.

And of course my mom, my mom loved to ride horses. She used to tell us about riding horses that would occasionally try to brush you off by rubbing against a fence or by walking you under a tree limb when they were tired of carrying you. Yeah, Momma had quite a passion for riding horses. She loved to go to church too. She was a Sunday school teacher and sang in the choir. In fact, I was in one of her Sunday school classes at a certain age. She made me behave too, by the way {laughs}. And you know, with eight children, she did not have time to take a walk. She stayed at home, preparing meals, washing clothes, cleaning the house. All of us pitched in and helped, but there was still all that work for mom to do and she did it. Even with all that, she always wanted to take time to study her Sunday school lesson. She was a Sunday school teacher down through the years, and so she kept busy and she liked to see us being kept busy also. But yes, she was the one who seemed to be more interested in going to church and taking part in it than Dad did, but Dad worked hard during the week. He did go to church, not every Sunday, but almost every Sunday, and he did participate and was an officer in the church. He was a deacon for a while. They believed in the church and loved Jesus and tried to get us to love Jesus and support our church as well.

Our family was a big, friendly family and we got along beautifully.

From the personal collection of Luther and Mary Masingill

Luther (fourth from left) with his family.

Of course they would discipline us if they had to, Momma and Daddy would. Daddy would whip us. He'd take his belt off and whip us. He was a big guy and he'd take off his belt and he'd whack us three or four times. And of course Momma, when she whipped us, she'd go out and get a hickory switch and she would be sure we felt it on our legs. That was our discipline back in those days. They don't do much of that anymore. If we did something during the day while daddy was at work and she did not want to whip us, she would say, "Your daddy will tend to you when he gets home." I would say, "Are you going to tell him? You don't have to tell him, do you?" I would ask nervously. "Yes, I have to tell him," she would say.

Over the years, Luther has mentioned various stories about his childhood and spending time with his family, especially his dad. I remember one story in particular when Luther and his dad went hunting with a friend named Mr. Epperson, who now works at the Chattanooga Funeral Home. Luther's dad and Mr. Epperson were hunting buddies and they took Luther with them one day. He was very little at the time and said they walked his "hind end off." He was so tired that his daddy had to carry him from way out in the woods all the way back to the car. So there was his dad, carrying Luther home while Mr. Epperson carried both guns.

Here are just a few other glimpses into Luther's childhood memories:

We grew up in the country in a place called King's Point overlooking the flat-lands that led right over to the Tennessee River. King's Point is out there around where the Coast Guard is now, way out in the country back in those days. Growing up, we had a very happy family. We all got along and I don't remember any real dissension. There were eight people in one house and the house was sufficient enough that we all had enough room. I do remember getting so cold, though, because we did not have any central heating back in those days. It would get so cold in wintertime that my momma and daddy would cover us up — a lot of times there'd be two or three of us in a bed — and cover us with blankets, homemade blankets, and I mean a lot of them. They were so thick you could hardly turn over, and they were so heavy. It was so cold in the room that if you had a glass of water on the table by your bedside, you'd find ice in it. Not solid, but you'd find ice in that glass the next morning. That's how cold it was.

I also remember we lived on the side and on top of a hill and it tapered off pretty fast. There was a pump down at the bottom of a hill. We all loved to go down with Momma or Daddy to pump enough water in the tank that was up above our house to last us all week for bathing and cooking. We'd start up the pump and it would pump out of the well underneath, enough water into that tank to last us a week, and then we'd have to go down and do it again the next Saturday.

One of the most exciting times was the landing of a plane near the house. It was a two- winged plane, a biplane, and the pilot ran out of gas and he landed in a cornfield. We watched him land and there was no damage. He got out of the plane and he had those unusual-looking, old-fashioned goggles on and he was wearing a cap and a leather jacket as he walked toward us. We were the only house in that area at the time. He said, "I'm looking for some gas." I think Daddy had some in a can in the garage and we gave him that. He wanted to pay us for it, but Momma wouldn't let him. So he took it and we got a nice letter from him about a week after that. I guess he was a pilot who had worked out of Lovell Field. That happened more than once, planes landing in that field. I don't know why that field just appealed to them. Maybe it looked kind of smooth. They would land and correct whatever problem they had and then fly on out of there.

One week when I was about seven or eight, we all got into our big four-door Dodge and we went to Kentucky to visit Mom's relatives. While we were there, we got a telegram stating our home had been destroyed by fire. I remember Daddy came in and he read it silently. We were all wondering what was in

it. Then he just turned and said, "We've got to go home. We've got to go home. Where our home was…it's burned. We've had a fire. Our home has burned." It sure was, man, right to the ground. So we moved in the garage. We had a garage that was a little bit larger than the average garage and so we moved into it. We lived in that garage until they built the house back. Then later, when I was somewhere around nine or ten years old, we moved to East Chattanooga, the Avondale area, down on Roanoke Street. It was Roanoke and Tinker, right across from the Avondale Baptist Church. Shortly thereafter, we moved over to Bradt Street, which was just behind Avondale Baptist Church.

Growing up in a family of eight children, you have to have a sense of humor. Luther says his family loved to laugh.

One of the many things I love about Luther is his sense of humor. Many people hear his serious side, his business side, on the radio. What they may not realize is how much of a joker he is, and the role humor has played in his life. I asked him where he thinks he got his humor from, and while he

From the personal collection of Luther and Mary Masingill

Luther (middle) and his brothers pose for a silly Easter photo.

attributes some of it to his father, he talks about how his mother had an appreciation for humor as well.

Momma was funny. She liked to tell jokes that she would hear in church meetings and when they would go and have a sewing circle or something. If she heard one, she would tell it and she'd preface it with, "I've got a joke." She always did think they were funny. "Now I've got a joke, now don't laugh at it, but I want you to laugh at it because it's funny," and she would tell the joke. I wish I could remember some of them because they were funny.

Momma was like Daddy. They both had a sense of humor. The whole family did, all eight of us, five boys and three girls, and we all found the funny things in life.

A lot of the time, we laughed at things we weren't supposed to laugh at and then had to apologize for doing it. For example, once we got into the peach orchard of the fellow next door. His name was Moon. Mr. Moon was a nice guy. We got into his peach orchard when we thought he was gone, but he was watching us from the kitchen window. We got some of his peaches, not too many, just five or six, but they sure were good. He came out and just blessed us out! "You boys, you Masingill boys! You just don't — do you know that's stealing? Now if you'd have asked me, I would have given you some, but I'm not going to give you any now that you've stolen them. Now that you've taken them, go ahead and eat them and don't you come back in my peach orchard again!"

There were things like that where we laughed and maybe shouldn't have.

Luther shared his mother and father's sense of humor and has always talked about his parents and his upbringing with great fondness. I realized for the first time that Luther's dad died just before he got his first job in radio. It was a job that would change the course of his entire life and, for a large part, define it. When Luther's father passed away at an early age due to cancer, it was a very critical time for their family. Luther was barely a young man when his father died.

From the personal collection of Luther and Mary Masingill

Luther (back row, center) with all of his siblings in 1941.

From the personal collection of Luther and Mary Masingill

Luther (back row, second from left) with his brothers in 1941.

From the personal collection of Luther and Mary Masingill

Luther (back row, fourth from left) with some of his siblings and his mother (front center) in the late 1930s.

From the personal collection of Luther and Mary Masingill

Luther (back row, left) with most of his siblings and his mother (front left).

From the personal collection of Luther and Mary Masingill

Luther (right) with two of his brothers in the late 1930s.

I was 16 years old when my father passed away. I was still in high school. As I've said, there were eight of us and, boy, we missed him. He was a joker and loved to make us laugh. We loved him; we really did. When Daddy died, I had been working for a service station, Bill Penney Service Station, and made a few bucks during junior high and high school. I began helping out with the family because Daddy had died and there was no other money coming in. I had to pitch in with what little I made and help with the expenses of the family. We had a sister who was still there and a younger brother still there.

As for the funeral, back in those days most of the activity took place in your house. The body is brought to the house and is on display there. Then the funeral was in the church, but it was a sad day at the house when you went through the room. There are a couple of days where people are visiting, and it was a sad day to see your daddy there, knowing that he couldn't say, "Hey, Luke, where you going?" That's what he called me, Luke, short for Luther. I just wanted to say, "Dad, I'm going to the store to get me a Nehi Grape."

These stories of Luther's life have fascinated me, the stories of his parents and the death of his father at such an early age. But how did a country boy from Tennessee end up where he is today, as a nationally recognized broadcasting legend? Luther's son Jeffrey says, "It's amazing to me that someone can have the same job for 70 years. People change jobs these days, sometimes because you have to or you get downsized or whatever, but to stay at the same job and do the same thing for 70 years, you have to love it. It's what he loves to do. I can remember my grandmother telling me as a kid that my dad would take a broomstick or he would take a can or a tin cup and put it on top of the broomstick. That was his mic and he would go around 'interviewing people.' The broomstick with the tin can on top was his microphone."

Whether childhood play or an unknown foreshadowing of the future, Luther's broomstick-and-tin-can microphone would one day become the real thing, and he was soon to begin his journey into broadcasting history.

3
Luther the Broadcaster

Having listened to Luther on WDEF all my life, I cannot imagine my childhood without radio. Luther did not grow up listening to radio. In fact, he had other dreams, such as discovering the countryside while working on the railroads. He's mentioned that as a young man he thought about traveling the country while working on a train, seeing the world from the window of a caboose while warming his hands on a hot stove. Fate had a very different path in mind for Luther, and it did not include the static, repetitious noise of train tracks, but a distinctive kind of noise. Luther remembers the first time he turned the dial, searching through the high-pitched sounds for a voice somewhere over the airwaves. He was about six or seven years old the first time he ever heard a radio station on the air.

The first radio I ever heard was WLW Cincinnati and the second station I ever heard was WSB Atlanta. I got them on a little crystal set and I thought that was fascinating. Daddy bought me a pair of earphones and you could hear, even though it was kind of weak, "Here's WLW Cincinnati, Ohio." The volume wasn't great and the quality of the signal was very low, but you could hear it. I thought, "That person is an adult and he's radio announcing in Cincinnati" (or Atlanta or whatever I was listening to), but again, you couldn't tell too much because of the signal strength. If you had a regular radio, you could get them. Both of those stations were

Personality · Dependability · Friendliness

LUTHER MASINGILL   BETTY JO BOWEN   DAVID REYNOLDS

EMILY JOHNSTON   AUBREY PENDERGRASS   ETHEL LEWIS

From the personal collection of Luther and Mary Masingill

Luther (top left) in his high school yearbook.

clear channel stations, AM, but they had a good strong signal. There were not very many other stations on the air, so they put out a strong signal. You could listen to Cincinnati radio down in New Orleans.

That was my first experience with radio and I was fascinated by it. I kept getting more interested in it all the time. While in junior high school, I was working at a service station on Dodson Avenue in Avondale called Bill Penney Tire and Marine. They had an intercom system between the tire recapping department warehouse and the regular part of the service station where you paid your bill for your gas and everything. I was always getting on that intercom system and saying things. One day, Bill Penney said, "I hear there's a radio station going to go on the air pretty soon. Why don't you look into it?" I said, "Okay, I'll do that." That same day Joe Engel, owner of the Chattanooga Lookouts baseball team, drove in to buy some gas. While I was wiping his windshield, I said, "Mr. Engel, I understand you are going to open a station." He said, "That's right, I'm going to. What's your name? You want a job?" I quickly answered, "Well shoot, yeah, Mr. Engel! I'll take a job. This windshield wiping is good but – "He stopped me and said, "Well, come on down. In fact, we're having auditions tonight." And I said, "Good. I'd like to have a job as – well, I've been thinking about asking for the job of answering the phone." At the time, they had all-request programs and I wanted to answer the phones. He said, "Well, uh, come on down tonight at 6:00." So that night I went down and I walked in his office and he said, "Take this copy and go in there and read it." I said, "No, Mr. Engel, I'm here for the telephone operator job during the part of the program where you have the all-request show." He said, "Oh, yeah, we can do that later. Let's try the radio and see how you sound. Here, take this copy and go on in there." So I took it into the studio and read it aloud without reading over it first. I read it and kicked a couple of words out and I could hear him laughing through two walls. Anyway, after it was over, he was there with his new manager and he said, "I'm looking for an apprentice announcer, a cub announcer. How would you like to be our cub announcer? You sounded pretty good in there and our manager here, he thinks you did too." I said, "Yeah, I'll give it a try, Mr. Engel, although I came down to answer the phone for your all-request program. That was what I had in mind, but yeah, I'll give it a try." So that's the way my radio career started many, many years ago.

From the personal collection of Luther and Mary Masingill

An early WDEF publication: "This is WDEF, Joe Engel's Station of
Public Service."

From the personal collection of Luther and Mary Masingill

Personality Man

"JOE ENGEL'S STATION"

Joe Engel, WDEF's owner, boasts of a career which has earned for him the name of "baseball's one man circus." Born in Virginia, Engel is known first for his interest in the sport, which evidenced itself when, as a boy he was sent to study the violin, but he regularly hid his instrument and joined the "felles" in a sand-lot game. His present activities include, in addition to the radio station, ownership of the Chattanooga "Lookouts" of the Southern Baseball Association. During the past year he has sold stock in the Club to fans at $5.00 the share. From scouting for the Griffith Washington team, Engel has become one of Chattanooga's most popular and respected citizens. Feeding the poor at the ball park on Christmas is an annual affair, and the Joe Engel "opening day" stunts have made history. The all-time minor league attendance record is held in Chattanooga with over 24,000 people in the stands on a single day . . . and Engel giving away FREE, a complete house and lot, with a car in the garage! Engel once chased Dizzy Dean from his park for walking out on a charity-fund game. Hobbies include dogs and racing pigeons. WDEF is his first radio venture.

An early WDEF publication: "Joe Engel's Station."

33

Central's Senior Class Holds Annual Gala Party at School

From the personal collection of Luther and Mary Masingill

King and queen for a night were Luther Masingill and Emily Johnston, who took the roles of King and Queen of Hearts at the annual senior class party at Central High School Friday night. The party followed the Valentine theme, with Fred Helms, class president, as master of ceremonies.

Luther as the "King of Hearts" at Central High School's Annual Gala Party. Luther Masingill and Emily Johnston were selected by secret ballot by attending students as "King and Queen of Hearts." As seen in this image, Luther was still in high school when he got his first job in radio.

Luther was 17 years old and still in high school the very first time he went live on the air. He was in his last year of school and he worked after class and into the evening. He would stay downtown after school and then work a night shift down in the Volunteer Building until about 9:30 or 10:00 o'clock. From there, he would go home and study before going to bed. The next morning he would get up, go to school, and do it all again. The radio station had its beginnings on the fourth floor of the Volunteer Building in downtown Chattanooga. Luther describes going on the air for the first time and what his thoughts were about being on the radio.

WDEF Radio signed on the air on New Year's Eve in 1940. The entire crew was there and we all played a part and had our own responsibilities. We were on the fourth floor of the Volunteer Building. The very first time I went on the air, that New Year's Eve in December 1940, I read a 30-second Kay's Jewelry commercial. Everything we did back then was live; there were no recorded commercials back then. As for being on the radio, I did not really think of it in terms of talking to thousands of people. At the time I was thinking about how much I would make – 15 dollars a week, golly {laughs}. I was just thinking about what 15 dollars would buy. But in terms of being on the radio, I thought it was a good job, and they had said I sounded pretty good on the intercom system that they were listening to me on. And so I thought, you know, I'll give this a try.

Photo courtesy of WDEF-TV Archives

One of Luther's early promotional photos for **WDEF** Radio.

Meet the Mikemen

Luther Masingill, WDEF: One of the up-and-at-'em boys who "hounds" employers into hiring 'em . . . was considered too young for radio announcing, but virtually made station hire him via dramatic audition . . . hung around s t u d i o, b e f o r e station took to air, as unofficial o d d- j o b man . . . came the day w h e n s t u d i o heads called in prospective announcers for auditions — Luther's name wasn't listed . . . when auditions were finished, the bosses s t a r t e d to leave the a u d i e n c e room, but were stopped by an unseen, unannounced voice—Luther's . . . he had slipped into audition room, prepared his script, and let go at the mike when others finished , . . impressed boss, who hired him part-time (while hero was attending school), later moving him to regular announcing job . . . graduated from Central High this spring . . . hopes to attend U. T. or U. C. . . . hobbies: Golf and dancing . . . called "Jitterbug" . . . 19, weighs about 150, 5 feet 10½ . . . ambition: Reach radio heights and have Sundays off.

MASINGILL

Image courtesy of WDEF-TV Archives

"Meet the Mikemen" featuring 19-year-old Luther at the dawn of his broadcasting career. His ambition was to "reach radio heights and have Sundays off."

MEET MR. KAY—Yessir, this is Luther Massengale, who is Mr. Kay of the popular radio team, the O. K. Boys. "Mr. Kay" is in charge of the radio department at the Kay Jewelry Company, 630 Market Street. Heard over WDEF from 12 to 12:15 daily, Mr. Kay suggests that his many friends visit him at the store any afternoon from now until Christmas. He says, "Yes, you can find me at Chattanooga's most popular jewelry—where it's O. K. to owe Kay."

Luther as "Mr. Kay" in an effort to promote and boost sales for the Kay Jewelry Company, where it was "O.K. to owe Kay."

Give it a try he did, and 72 years later, he is still going strong, working for the same station, WDEF, that he started at as a kid in high school. Fifteen dollars a week must have seemed like a lot back then, especially since Luther's dad died early in his life and Luther was helping provide for his family. Like many young men at the time, he was also drafted into the military. Luther has a longstanding joke that he often tells when asked about the war.

I fought and fought and I still had to go {laughs}. No, it really sunk in that I was going off to war when I was drafted. I believe it was December of 1942. It was a fairly cold day on a Sunday afternoon and they had to light up a stove there in

Fort Oglethorpe, which is where we ended up after getting in a big old Army truck at the downtown Hamilton County Courthouse. I got in that truck with a bunch of guys from Alabama, Georgia, and other parts of Tennessee who were instructed to be there.

The next morning they started giving us tests. They put us all in a room with a hundred typewriters, and all these people that came in with me had never even seen a typewriter before. I was the only one in that class of a hundred that had typing experience. I had just gotten out of high school and I had some typing experience. I had made a good grade, and when I got through, they said, "All you guys are dismissed except — what's your name? Masingill? Masingill. Okay." So everybody left the room. He said, "Okay, Masingill, we're going to make a clerk out of you." I said, "Wait a minute; I don't want to be a clerk." He quickly responded by asking, "What do you want to be?" I knew he was not willing to help me when I asked, "Do I have a choice? I'd like to get into communications in the Signal Corp. I'm in radio business right now." Skeptically, he replied, "Well, I don't know." About that time a gentleman came out of the barracks office and said, "Luther!" I recognized him because he worked in the same building that I did, the Volunteer Building, and he was a warrant officer already in the service. I think he was drafted too. He said, "Luther, what are they trying to do to you?" I told him they wanted to make a clerk out of me and put me in quartermaster. He said, "Well, what do you want?" I told him I wanted Signal Corp, and he said, "Let me have those papers." He grabbed the papers and went back, and I'll always remember the sound of the rubber stamp — Boom! Boom! — on the desk. He brought the papers back out and said, "Alright, Luther, you are now in the Signal Corp and you're leaving tomorrow morning for Camp Crowder in Missouri." And I said, "What? Thank you and have a nice day!" The next day I was on a train headed to Camp Crowder.

LUTHER SIGNS OFF — A more powerful wave-length offering larger audience, is greater possibilities, and a much larger audience is to get the services of Luther Masingill, well-known WDEF announcer, shown above. Luther signed off today to join the armed forces at Fort Oglethorpe.

Luther has been with Joe Engel since the opening of the station and has developed into one of the best announcers in the South.

Engel claims he discovered Masingill as a filling station attendant in East Chattanooga. On the other hand, Luther claims he discovered Joe Engel. The argument has never been definitely settled, there being those who believe both sides.

Anyway, the Lookout prexy, who doubles in radio during the off season, admits he has always been very fond of the former Central High lad and, like the rest of us who know him, predicts that the young announcer will win many friends with his very fine personality. WDEF loses a valuable man . . . but to a very worthy cause.

(That should hold you, lad . . . and good luck, always.—E. T. B.)

Image courtesy of WDEF-TV Archives

Luther "signs off" to join the armed forces.

Image courtesy of WDEF-TV Archives

IN THE ARMY NOW

Luther Masingill, announcer for radio station WDEF, will leave Monday for duty in the army having been inducted this week at Fort Oglethorpe. He has been with WDEF since its establishment two years ago.

Luther "in the army now," December 18, 1942.

Before Luther was drafted, he says he never thought about being at WDEF for the rest of his life. When he began his radio career, he never really thought very far ahead regarding his future. He was just a young teenager and did not think that way. When he was drafted and hopped into that Army truck and was heading off to war, he thought it would be practical, having been in radio at the time, if he could get into some kind of communications. All he could do at the time was hope for a job in communications while he was in the service. Even though it was on a limited scale, he did think it was enjoyable to get into the Signal Corp. Luther learned a lot while he was in the military and discusses what it was like in the early days in communications while he was in the service and some of the changes that have taken place.

Image courtesy of WDEF-TV Archives

Luther and his three brothers were featured in a weekly layout by *The Chattanooga Times* highlighting local service men, Sunday, June 10, 1945.

During WWII when I was in the Admiralty Islands, just south of the Philippine Islands, I was introduced to a wire recorder. I was in the United States Signal Corps attached to the 13th Air Force, and we were their communication link. That is where I learned code – dot-dot ditty-ditty dot-dot dit-dit-dit dot. This wire recorder was on a little spool of wire. It was a funny-looking little thing but it had a fairly good sound – a little crispy. When I got back, our radio station was using them, in addition to disks they had been using for recording, which you actually cut with a needle. After that, of course, came the tapes. Tape was made of coated paper. The first tapes were on reels. Then they went to something like a plastic sort of material, and you know what happened after that, as technology just continued to get better and better.

From the personal collection of Luther and Mary Masingill

Luther in New Guinea while serving in the Signal Corp in 1943. He still uses a typewriter like the one seen in this photo for his radio show preparation today.

Luther has seen so much change over the years. He has been a witness to so many transformations in the broadcasting industry and has adapted to most of them. One change Luther has refused to make is upgrading from his famous Royal typewriter. He began using a Royal typewriter in high school, used the same typewriter while in the service, and still uses the same kind today.

I love my Royal typewriter. It's not the same typewriter that I used in the early days, of course, but the same model and everything. It's the model I used in high school and the one I used on top of a hill in Buna, Papua New Guinea, in a communications tent with some screened wiring. The bugs still managed to get in that tent, the kind of bugs you find in the jungle, but yes, that was it. I've kept the same typewriter all these years because I just like the touch of it, the feel of it. I love that old typewriter. I really do.

I've seen the picture many times of Luther as a young man in New Guinea during WWII with his Royal typewriter. Occasionally, he has mentioned some of his experiences during the war, and I asked him if he still thinks about it today.

Mary and I have talked about it. Something about the service would come up or there would be a news story about somewhere in the Philippines, and she would ask me if I was there. I served in the Philippines. In fact, I was there when the war ended and I left from Palawan Island and came back home. Every once in a while somebody will stop me and say, "Luther, you probably don't remember this, but I met you on the ship that took us from San Francisco to Brisbane, Australia. I ate with you in the mess hall one day and we talked briefly about Chattanooga." Things like that come up in your lifetime, living 90 years or more, and you will run into people who remember you. Thank goodness it's fondly, and they get a laugh out of something you said or something you remember. Of course they are flattered if you remember their name. In one or two cases I remembered their name. It was somebody that I barely knew but I happened to remember their name.

From the personal collection of Luther and Mary Masingill

Luther (left) while serving in Papua New Guinea in 1942.

Chattanooga Evening Times, Tuesday, October 14, 1941.

But there are some things you see in wartime. You see the results of being shot, of being shot by a sniper. A sniper shoots somebody next to you on a lonely island in the Philippines, or wherever we were stationed at the time, and you see death. You see the look on the person's face. I've seen this the second they were shot. They knew they were shot and they knew that it was serious. I think in two or three cases, I remember it was the look of, "I'm going to die. That shot I just received in the chest is going to kill me. I won't see my family again." That's what you think of so many times, they tell me, people who have been shot. You wonder how your relatives are going to react to the news of your death. A lot of the time, you pull through and you're so happy about that and you tell them of that instance when you get home: "Hey, when I thought I was dying, I thought of you." But you do think of home and you do think of people you love.

Fortunately, Luther made it out of WWII and came home to Chattanooga. He did not have his morning show slot before he was drafted to fight in WWII. He did afternoon and evening work after school and did not have his morning program until he came back from the service.

What's Your Request?

From the personal collection of Luther and Mary Masingill

Luther and A.B. "Vann" Campbell in early WDEF promotional material.

*I was only on the air a short time before I was drafted and fought in WWII –
a year, two years at the most. Back then, radio was it. That was how you got your
news about what was going on in the world, through radio. Of course the newspapers did a good job too. But the radio…people had their radios on all the time.*

When I came back, I did a morning program with a guy name A.B. "Vann" Campbell who had two or three voices that he used. We had a lot of fun. "Vann" Campbell. I remember him very well, and he was a good guy to work with and that was our first morning show. We did a two-man show. He did voices in the morning and he had two or three voices he would use and I never would know which one he was going to use. When a client would get him on the phone for something on the air, I never knew which voice he was going to use.

At the beginning, when you first start out in radio and with no television exposure, of course you're not that well known. If they see you, they might recognize your voice if you say something to them. Of course, they did not have supermarkets back then, and so down at the corner store, if somebody heard your voice, they might recognize it and say, "Well you're on the radio aren't you, Fella?" "Yeah, I'm on the radio," I would say.

When I did come home from the war, I was greeted with a one-page ad in the newspaper that said, "Luther is back! After two and one-half years in the Pacific, Masingill is back home waking you up at 7:15 each morning, Monday thru Saturday. Bobby Soxers, their Ma's and Grandma's, are reminded that Luther is back – back at the same old stand – at the same old time!" It was nice to be greeted with a one-page ad in the newspaper for your homecoming from the war.

After Luther returned from the service and was greeted warmly by Chattanooga, he returned to his radio career in full force and his popularity continued to grow. In fact, Luther became so popular, he once ran for "mayor" of Chattanooga.

We were just trying to create some interest in the election. There really wasn't much attention being paid; nobody was really excited, not even those who were running in the election. I don't think they had much money to spend. Maybe that was the reason. You did not see or hear as much advertising, and so the station manager thought it was a good idea to jazz it up a little bit. "You run, Luther, and then withdraw right toward the end at the time when you can legally withdraw, and we'll create some interest." So I promised them everything: "I'll find your dog if you vote for me! Meet me Saturday down at the Krystal and I will buy you a hamburger. I'll make your kids go to bed on time!" I just promised all kinds of crazy stuff. Gosh, I would promise whatever popped into my mind, and people were like, "Listen to that crazy guy!"

From the personal collection of Luther and Mary Masingill

He's Back, Mr. Hooper!

"Luther" is Back!

After two and one-half years in the Pacific, Masingill is back home waking you up at 7:15 each morning, Monday thru Saturday.

Bobby Soxers, their Ma's and Grandma's, are reminded that Luther is back—back at the same old stand—at the same old time!

Tune for "Luther"—7:15-8:10 A.M.
Monday thru Saturday

WDEF
1400   ABC

*C. E. Hooper measures the ratings of most major stations and networks.

Luther is welcomed back to WDEF "after two and one-half years in the Pacific." *The Chattanooga Times*, Sunday, January 27, 1946.

Chattanooga News-Free Press, Monday, March 5, 1951.

Promises 'Anything' . . .

Luther Masingill Has More Fun Than 'Real' Mayor Candidates

By J. B. COLLINS

Luther Masingill, popular young radio announcer, isn't really serious about his candidacy for mayor in the coming city primary, but he's having more fun with his frivolous campaign than all the serious candidates combined.

Regularly on his two daily programs—"Sun Dial" in the mornings and "Loafin' With Luther" in the afternoons on station WDEF—Luther chirps, sings, cajoles and shouts about his candidacy.

He has reached a new high in burlesquing politicians. He has promised everything in the books and some things that aren't there. Hardly any of his promises are even remotely associated with the mayor's office to which he "aspires," but that never stumps the effervescent Luther.

He started his campaign early, several weeks ago. He began by dealing lightly with a rather ticklish real situation—the location of the new tunnel through Missionary Ride.

'M'CALLIE CANYON'

"Why," declared Luther over one of his popular recording programs, "if you elect me mayor I'll settle the tunnel question once and for all. I'll dig out the McCallie Avenue Tunnel completely and run five lanes through the gap—four lanes for traffic and one for wrecks. I'll call it the McCallie Canyon."

His public caught on fast and "beefs" about everything in general began coming in to Luther by mail and telephone. Luther promptly promised to clear up every one. He's promised everything but the moon, and that'll probably be next.

He's even promised jobs over at city hall.

"I think I'll make my mother sidewalk inspector," he said in pear-shaped tones. "She comes into town about twice a week so she'll be able to take care of that job all right."

'DOG CATCHER ENGEL'

He has promised the dog catcher's job to Joe Engel, Luther's former boss and now full-time president of the Chattanooga Lookouts baseball team.

Among his more popular promises are to:

● Build a 12-lane bridge across the Tennessee River—six lanes to enter Broad Street and six to enter Market Street.

● Dig out Stringer's Ridge Tunnel, making a canyon, and give everybody who votes for him a free load of dirt.

● Get every old maid a husband —his motto being "a man for every house." (He's a bachelor himself.)

● Buy a large area ouside the city so that gas, water and telephone companies and the streets and sewers department can dig to their heart's content instead of digging up streets and sidewalks.

● Get prices for haircuts reduced for balding men.

● Eliminate railroad crossings in downtown area.

● Give everyone a straight telephone line at party-line prices.

He includes some other promises that make present officials somewhat uneasy, like a bonus for every veteran, removal of the $5 auto sticker and all parking meters, and salary increases for teachers.

He doesn't say where he's going to get the money. He says he'll worry about that when he's mayor.

'CAMPAIGN FUND'

Mayor Wasson, going along with the joke, sent Luther $2.03 for his "campaign fund." Masingill, not to be outdone, promptly bought some cardboard and, using his own press, printed himself a couple of thousand political cards.

Luther is worried only about one thing. He's afraid that there'll be some folks who will go along with his fun campaign to the extent of writing in his name on the ballot.

But on this he is serious. "I hope nobody will do that," he said. "They would be sacrificing their right to vote for their choice of the legitimate candidates."

But Luther is going right ahead with his promise campaign. If you want anything, just call Luther. You probably will never get it, but he'll promise it to you.

"And," Luther observes, "after all these things, if there is any money left, I plan to pave the driveway of everyone in the city —just vote for me for mayor!!"

Luther had more fun than the real mayoral candidates, making outlandish promises like giving his mother the job of sidewalk inspector and "prices for haircuts reduced for balding men."

News-Free P

Luther for Mayor

Mr. Friddell Wants Native of City to Hold Top Position

To The Chattanooga News-Free Press:

To all Chattanoogans:

In regard to the upcoming political race for the office of mayor of Chattanooga, let's get Chattanooga back into the hands of Chattanoogans. There are to many outsiders running Chattanooga's business, people who don't really care for the people of Chattanooga, whose main purpose for seeking public office is to upgrade themselves and degrade Chattanoogans.

However, there is a solution for this problem and here is my interpretation. There is a man born and reared here in Chattanooga and still living in Chattanooga who would make the finest mayor Chattanooga has ever had. Every man, woman and child in the Chattanooga area knows this man. Mr. Chattanooga himself, Luther Masingill! He knows more about Chattanooga's sorrows and woes and its gladness and joys than any other Chattanoogan.

So let's not hire a foreigner to head up our city government. We owe it to this fine civic leader of our city in appreciation for his past and present and future efforts of making Chattanooga a better place to live.

Let's vote for and elect Luther Masingill mayor of Chattanooga.

WOODROW FRIDDELL.

Image courtesy of WDEF-TV Archives

A listener writes to the paper to urge citizens to vote for "Mr. Chattanooga himself, Luther Masingill!"

To Luther

Says Mayor's Job Easier
To Fill Than His

To The Chattanooga News-Free Press:

To Luther Masingill:

I am writing you with reference to your running for mayor of our fine city. Luther, I hope you will give this matter a great deal of consideration. No doubt you would make Chattanooga one of the finest mayors we have ever had as you are a very dedicated man loved by us all. I am well aware that our city could stand a few changes but it happens so many times that a job of this nature, where politics are involved, changes the man taking office, and Luther we do not want anything to change you or shatter your image with all your thousands of friends and good listeners, particularly the children who would all go around with a mouth full of cavities because Luther wouldn't be around to remind them to brush their teeth. It would even be sad for the dogs, all wondering around lost, trying to find their way back home.

So, the way I see it, it would be much easier to fill the mayor's chair than it would Luther's. So, keep the job that will never need a replacement.

BETTY L. BEAVERS,
736 Moore St.

A devoted listener writes to the paper to declare that it "would be much easier to fill the mayor's chair than it would Luther's."

Fun Race Over, Luther Says 'Vote for Real Candidates'

"The fun is over—now let's get serious."

That's the way Luther Masingill, popular radio announcer, feels about his fun campaign for mayor.

For a couple of months now Luther has appealed for votes over his two daily radio programs, promising everything . . . anything. His audience went along, laughing at his promises to "get every old maid a husband, dig a five-lane (one for wrecks) canyon through Missionary Ridge, build a 12-lane bridge across the river, buy a large lot out in the country so that gas and water employes can 'dig to their hearts' content'."

Although it was all in fun, some of his promises caused some of the present officials to stir uneasily, apparently wondering if the voters thought that maybe they should be doing some of the things Luther was promising to do.

One city employe, apparently feeling he was carrying the brunt of one of Luther's platform planks, asked Luther and Luther's boss to go easy. Luther gladly obliged, pointing out that it was not his intention to embarrass anyone.

Luther said he hoped that none of the legitimate candidates was displeased with his campaign. He said he felt that Mayor Wasson apparently enjoyed his campaign as much as anyone. Luther said Wasson twice sent him (small) donations to finance his campaign in response to Luther's concern over having to scrape the bottom of his campaign barrel.

Wasson added a postscript to his last letter in which a donation was sent: "If you don't win, Luther, I hope I do."

But Luther is calling a sudden halt to his fun campaign. He doesn't want anyone to lose his vote because of his "running for mayor." He pointed out that his objective in starting his campaign was to stimulate interest in the election and to help get out a heavy vote.

His plea for his friends to vote for a legitimate candidate appears elsewhere in this edition in a full-page ad in which he urged the folks to "vote for Luther"—for good entertainment, not for mayor.

"The fun is over – now let's get serious," urges Luther as he encourages citizens to "vote for real candidates."

Of course right toward the end of the campaign, I pulled out and said, "No, no, don't vote for me, I was only joking. Vote for one of the other candidates. Give them your vote and put them in there and they will do a good job." Before I withdrew, I think some of the other candidates were worried that I might get it, and they talked the station manager into kind of hurrying up my withdrawal a little bit. "Get him out of there," they said. And I would see some of the candidates at various places where they were making an appearance. I would just happen by and they would come over and put their arm around me and wish me luck. This was before I withdrew. They were a couple of nice guys. One of them was with the Colonial Bakery, the one who became mayor, Mayor Olgiatti. That's how we started a friendship. I got my bread at a discount and he was good to me as a mayor.

With Luther's longevity at WDEF Radio, people often think he owns the station or that he's my boss. People are constantly asking what it's like to have Luther as a boss. Jokingly I tell them, "Well, he's a pretty good boss; he's okay." They seem to think that since he's Luther, he can say anything he wants to without consequence. I asked Luther if it's as easy as he makes it look, or if he's ever had any challenges when it comes to talking on the air.

There are good days and bad days of course. There was coming back from the war and receiving that greeting with the one-page ad in the newspaper. That was a really good day, but as for bad days, or challenging situations, I remember right at the beginning we had a very strict manager.

He was very strict and very business-like, but he had his lighter moments also about calling you down on something you may have said on the air. "Luther," he would say, "I don't believe I would have worded it quite that way." I said, "Tell me how you would have done it." And of course he'd tell me. I always knew that he did

From the collection of Luther and Mary Masingill

Luther as a young man when he was first getting started in radio.

not care for certain references to certain situations, but he made his point clear. It was little things I'd say that did not amount to too much and he did not make a big to-do out of it. He'd just say it was better if I used this term or that term. Overall, he was good to me and he was a good manager. He had a good secretary and she took care of everything and told him when he had meetings with officials from the city. He'd be there and he'd come back that day and pass the word along to us about what the city officials were expecting of WDEF, 1370 on the dial at the time. We were AM on the dial. We hadn't gone to FM yet. That was in the 1940s. I came back from the service in the late '40s — '45, '46 — right in there. Man, the years sure have gone by fast.

Ever since Luther began his radio career many years ago, he has had an engineer, someone who controls the audio equipment and regulates volume and sound quality during a broadcast. Luther has always sat in front of the microphone after generating a list of music and stacking records. When he began, that's what the music was played on — records. Of course technology has changed drastically over the years, but Luther began his career with an engineer and continues to use one today.

Photo courtesy of WDEF-TV Archives

Luther in his early days of radio.

They always gave me an engineer who did the playing of the records, the playing of the tapes, the playing of the disks that were recorded by the station or somebody local. I had an engineer who did all of that and set it up. I'd point to him and he'd hit the recording or the tape or whatever it was at the time. I'd stack the music and give it to him and give him a list and he'd go by that list. That's back when we played adult contemporary music, "easy listening" I think it was called then, "beautiful music," but "adult contemporary" now.

The way technology has changed is just amazing. I've explained many times in interviews how, when I went into the service, the station had disks that we recorded on, fairly big wide disks. Actually, a needle cut into it as you recorded something and that was there at the station when I left. In the service, when we were in the Signal Corp, they made taping and recording equipment available to us. We had wire recorders, a spool of wire, not very big but that would record whatever you wanted to record. I came back home and some of the radio stations were using wire recorders. A short time later, they went to tape, to paper tape, a coated paper tape. And then a short time later, they went to a plastic tape that was a lot more efficient and the quality was a lot better than the paper tape. Then we went right on down to videotape, a big, wide spool of tape. They finally got it down to where you could carry it in your hand to a program or an event; you could carry it, push a button, and it will transmit for you to the station, and they in turn broadcast it for you. There are just so many amazing things. I cannot recall all of them right now but so many things and so beautifully done over the years in radio and television. It's been great to see all the changes.

While technology continues to change and evolve, one thing that hasn't changed over the years is Luther's personality and what he means to his local community. I've watched many times, as we've been out at different station events, the way people respect and revere Luther and what he means as a broadcaster to the people of Chattanooga. He's a celebrity, and as humble as he is, he is truly a living legend in the business of broadcasting. But to Luther, it's not about fame or being a celebrity, it is about his philosophy of helping people. He uses his broadcasting career as a method to help others in some way. He strives to do whatever is within his power to improve the lives of those around him and within the sound of his voice. Luther contributes the longevity of his career to this attitude and this is how he continues to think about his job to this day. In July of 2012, Steve Hartman from CBS News in New York came to Chattanooga to do a feature on Luther for the *On The Road* series.

Photo by Holly Abernathy

Luther and CBS News correspondent Steve Hartman as they look back over photos from Luther's early days in broadcasting, July 2012.

Photo by Holly Abernathy

Luther shows CBS News correspondent Steve Hartman and associate producer Miles Doran how they used to record "in the old days," July 2012.

Photo by Holly Abernathy

Sunny 92.3 WDEF morning show co-host Kim Lyons Carson alongside CBS News associate producer Miles Doran and CBS News correspondent Steve Hartman. James Howard speaks to Mr. Hartman live on the air about their visit to Chattanooga to highlight the career of Luther Masingill, July 2012.

Photo by Holly Abernathy

James Howard and Gene Lovin, part of the Sunny 92.3 WDEF morning show crew, with CBS News correspondent Steve Hartman and associate producer Miles Doran. CBS News featured Luther on the 6:30 national evening news highlighting his unprecedented career and his place in broadcasting history, July 2012.

Photo by Holly Abernathy

The Sunny 92.3 WDEF morning show crew (Gene Lovin, Luther Masingill, James Howard, Kim Lyons Carson) with CBS News correspondent Steve Hartman (center), July 2012.

During the interviews with Steve Hartman, Luther's philosophy of helping people was evident in his answers to Steve's probing questions. Here is what Luther had to say after the CBS crew visited the WDEF Radio studios:

That Steve Hartman is a young whippersnapper {laughs}. I love the way he takes command with his photographers. He has done a good job while working here in Chattanooga. I have enjoyed working with him and I think he has enjoyed listening to the stories of old time radio and what it was like years ago. One of the questions he asked me was about the different offers I've received over the years and why I turned them down. A while back, I had quite a few offers from L.A., New York, Philadelphia, places like that. I told him I was flattered, but I did not want to leave. I love this town. He said, "Did you love it that much that you passed up a good increase in salary?" I said, "Yeah, I do." He put the questions to me. He said, "You're famous here for lost dogs and cats. Wouldn't you like to be known for something a little more important than that?" "No," I said, "dogs and cats are important to people, they love them, and I try to help them find them. It's just a part of the program."

For me, it's always been about helping people. And as far as any celebrity or fame, there is a certain amount of that that comes with it, and of course it's flattering, that look on a person's face as they approach you in a supermarket or in a shopping mall or parked at an intersection. They look over and you can read their lips. They are saying to the person with them, "That's Luther!" So you wave and smile. My good friend Buddy Houts used to get tickled about that. We'd be driving along and we'd stop at an intersection and people would do that. They'd recognize both of us and he would say, "Hey! We're both famous! Did you notice that? They recognized us!" Then he wanted to race them, but he never did. Buddy loved to race cars {laughs}.

At the beginning there wasn't too much fame or celebrity. Of course, television helped so much with that. I went into that in 1954 when WDEF Channel 12 went on the air, but people knew me from radio. They did not quite put the name with the face, but then if they heard me, they'd say, "Yeah, you're on the radio; you're Luther!" Later with television, they were able to put a face with that voice and they'd say, "Oh you're on radio and television." I said, "Yeah, I sure am and I appreciate you tuning in." You always thank them for tuning in, and I started making a habit of saying, "By the way, if you ever lose your dog or your cat, call me." They always thought that was funny.

Most people here in the Tennessee Valley know Luther by his face or voice, but his name is also synonymous with pets, lost pets.

Photo courtesy of WDEF-TV Archives

Luther is well known for helping people find their lost pets, September 1986.

Ever since I was a kid, and of course after my own experience with my lost dog Andy, I wondered how Luther became known as a lost dog advocate. Not only is he known for his heart and his kindness to others, he's also known for finding lost dogs and cats. We get many calls in the morning, and most people don't realize that in January and July when there are fireworks, Luther will have 25 phone calls about lost or found pets. So the majority of the morning show in January and July is about lost dogs. We get a lot of phone calls from people from out of town or just passing through saying they've never heard of anything like this before. With all the growth happening in the Chattanooga area, we have many people who come from different areas saying, "Who is this Luther? We've never heard of anything like this before." I remember one story that made the newspaper. A couple had come down from Michigan, and they lost their dog while they were here. They had to get back home, yet they were still unable to find their dog. They kept calling Luther once a week from Michigan until Luther was able to find their dog. It was a wonderful reunion for them. Luther is definitely one-of-a-kind. When it comes to finding lost pets, it just sort of happened.

In my early days of radio in the 1940s, I played mostly music and weather and little news bits, you know. I started getting into lost dogs, not many back in those days, one or two on a program. But it just kept growing and showing popularity and finally I was known as a lost dog man. The first call I received was somewhere around 1945 or '46, after I got back from the service. Someone called me, and before the conversation ended, they were in tears and I could hardly understand them because of the depth of their grief. And I thought, man, people really love their animals. I had a dog at the time named Rex and I loved him too, so I thought that this would be a really good way to help people. So I said, "Well, let's see if we can help you find it on the air." So I mentioned it and the response was so amazing that they found their dog in just a few minutes after I put it on the air. So the word got around that if you lost your dog, call this guy Luther. Luther, he'll help you find your dog. So it grew and the word passed around — if you lose your dog or your cat or your horse or your cow. I've reported all these things.

Luther's daughter Joan recalls her dad's reaction to the mistreatment of an animal: "I can tell you the angriest I have ever seen my dad get was one time – we all saw it – when this young boy was mistreating a dog. I honestly have never seen him so angry when he went and he got the dog and brought it home. If I remember correctly, he went to the boy's home and spoke with his mother or grandmother. I remember it was one of those times where you go, 'Yeah, Dad! Go!' I was probably 12 or 13, and of course we are animal lovers, but I had just never seen him get that passionate or that angry about something. He just was not going to put up with that and he did not."

I asked Luther if there is one story in particular that sticks out in his mind about finding a lost pet for someone.

I remember in North Chattanooga a woman called and said, "Luther, I've lost my two Jack Russell terriers. I said, "Okay I'll put it on the air." A woman just two blocks away was washing dishes in the kitchen and looked out the window and there were the two Jack Russell terriers. I had given the owner's name and address on the air, and she knew the woman, so she called her right away. "Honey, I've got your dogs. I heard Luther talking about it on the air, and I've got your dogs." The owner told her she would be right over, but the lady said, "No, no, I'm getting ready to leave the house. I've got a shopping trip, so I'll just put them in the back of the car and bring them over." The owner agreed and told the woman she appreciated that very much. So the woman put them in the car and went over – it was a hot summer day, by the way – and she drove up in front of the house. She told me that, as she drove up to the house, the owner came out on the front porch, down the steps, and was heading toward the car at the same time she was getting out of her car. She got out as the owner came out of her house to greet her, but the dogs were left in the car. As soon as she got out of the car, the dogs locked it! The dogs had become so excited after seeing their owner that they had pushed down the door locks in the car. The owner was just frantic. She could see her dogs in the car and she couldn't get them out. The owner couldn't get them out because the only other key was in the pocket of her husband who had just flown to San Francisco that morning. They finally had to call the locksmith to get the doors open and get the dogs out. The dogs were enjoying it though. It was cool in there with the air conditioning on because it was a hot summer day. They were more comfortable than the people outside.

Yes, over the years, I have found cows, snakes, alligators, horses, ponies and one llama. The llama had gotten loose down around the Lookout Valley area. Over the years, you will find you have the opportunity to find all kinds of animals that people have taken on as pets. Somehow they get out and get away from them. Over the years, I've never seen such a love for animals. They just really love them, and if something happens to them, call Luther. He'll try to help you find it. A lot of times we're lucky and we do help them find them, the animal that they love so much.

Of course Luther is well known for his love of pets and for helping people find their lost animals, but Luther has also been recognized for one of the most amazing careers in the history of broadcasting. He has received numerous awards and recognition for things he has done over the years, including the prestigious Marconi Award in 1990 from the National Association of Broadcasters. One of the most amazing moments in my career alongside Luther was when the city approved a portion of South Broad Street in Chattanooga to be renamed "Luther Masingill Parkway".

Photo by Holly Abernathy

James and Luther on the day a portion of South Broad Street in Chattanooga became "Luther Masingill Parkway," August 2010.

Part of Broad Street named for radio's Luther Masingill

By Barry Courter
BCOURTER@TIMESFREEPRESS.COM

Motorists now can listen to radio personality Luther Masingill as they drive along a stretch of Broad Street named in his honor.

The 3200 block of the street was renamed Luther Masingill Parkway during an unveiling ceremony Thursday at Mt. Vernon Restaurant.

The section of road covers a half mile of Broad Street on either side of the studios of WDEF, where Masingill has worked for 70 years in both radio and television.

"It is truly appropriate that he is honored this way given the number of lives he has impacted over the

Luther Masingill

years," said state Sen. Bo Watson, R-Hixson.

Watson proposed the legislation to rename the road in honor of Masingill in April, and it was passed by the Tennessee Legislature.

Known mainly as Luther, Masingill said he was humbled by the honor and joked with the gathered crowd of politicians, reporters, co-workers and friends as he, along with some help from Chattanooga Mayor Ron Lit-

tlefield who worked to peel a stubborn layer of protective plastic off, revealed the new sign carrying his name.

"It really is an honor after all of these years," Masingill said. "You don't get a lot of honors in radio and to get something like this is really special."

Littlefield called the ceremony a "celebration of a long journey. It has been long discussed to honor Luther."

He said renaming a street after someone is not done very often, but this was the right thing to do.

Image courtesy of WDEF-TV Archives

Luther's wife, Mary, was also proud of her husband for this honor. "They are naming a street after you? I thought you had to be dead before they did that!" she jokingly said. "It was exciting because you see little areas of town where the streets have been named after different people and I thought, 'That is as good as it gets in Chattanooga.' It's wonderful to be able to enjoy seeing the street named after you. We appreciated the senator that brought it up. People have just been so good to Luther. He has given back to the city through his time and voice, but it is an honor to be acknowledged for what you do."

I was extremely proud of Luther as well and was privileged to take part in the event. I have to admit I thought it was long overdue, and it really did not surprise me. I had the opportunity to speak the day that the city, the county, and a few others bestowed the honor on him. I was able to share my admiration of Luther when I was a kid. I was proud of him because, in my opinion, he deserved to have the *city* named after him. I stood at the podium and looked out over all the broadcasters that were present, including David Carroll that I remembered watching as a child, as well as some of the management of WDEF-Television and Radio. Of course, it was a pleasure being in front of my employer and my bosses and to have them hear my heart when it comes to how much I love Luther. It was a privilege to be in the same room as Luther and to be right next to him as a broadcaster, especially at the moment when such a high honor was bestowed upon him. Luther had this to say about that day:

The naming down on Broad Street was an honor. It's just a small section down there on South Broad Street, a little section from the radio station down to the end of Broad, down by Mt. Vernon Restaurant. That was an honor. They had a little ceremony, and I climbed a ladder and pulled the wrapping off of the sign. We had a good time that day. Yes, that's another honor that I appreciate.

Below is a copy of the bill that was passed regarding Luther Masingill Parkway:

Public Chapter No. 822 PUBLIC ACTS, 2010 1
PUBLIC CHAPTER NO. 822
SENATE BILL NO. 2643
By Watson, Berke, Ford
Substituted for: House Bill No. 2715
By Brown, Favors, Dean, McCormick, Floyd, Jim Cobb, Shaw
AN ACT to name a segment of Broad Street in the City of Chattanooga in honor of
beloved broadcaster, Luther Masingill.

WHEREAS, from time to time, the members of this General Assembly have seen fit to name certain highways and bridges to honor those exemplary public servants who have contributed significantly to the growth and prosperity of their respective communities; and

WHEREAS, one such noteworthy person is Mr. Luther Masingill, who has been a fixture on WDEF Radio in Chattanooga for nearly seventy years and a vital part of WDEF Television since it began broadcasting in 1954; he has earned both the Tennessee Association of Broadcaster's Distinguished Service Award and the coveted Marconi Award for his professional excellence; and

WHEREAS, Mr. Masingill's longstanding tenure in radio broadcasting began on New Year's Eve 1940; nearly seven decades later, Luther continues to proudly serve the listeners of WDEF; and

WHEREAS, the "longest running radio announcer on the same station in the U.S.," Mr. Masingill is the only current broadcaster in America to have announced the news of both the terrorist attacks on September 11, 2001, and the attack on Pearl Harbor on December 7, 1941; and

WHEREAS, Mr. Masingill acts as a true friend to all of his listeners on his morning drive radio show; from finding bus schedules for listeners to reporting problems like potholes, missing street signs, and locations of needed traffic signals to city officials, he is never "too busy" to offer his assistance; and

WHEREAS, a member of America's greatest generation and a World War II veteran, Mr. Masingill also remains active on WDEF Television, doing his daily Community Calendar on the morning show, his ever popular "Dog Gone" segment on the noon news, and his "Life with Luther" feature on the evening news; and

WHEREAS, an active and devoted member of his community, Mr. Masingill is credited with reuniting more animals with their owners than the City Humane Society, finding clothing and furniture for families who have lost their homes to fire, and finding heaters or air conditioning units for those in need; and

Public Chapter No. 822 PUBLIC ACTS, 2010 2

WHEREAS, this General Assembly finds it appropriate to name a segment of the Chattanooga street that is home to WDEF, namely Broad Street, in honor of Luther

Masingill as a token of our esteem for him, both as a broadcaster and as a citizen; now, therefore,

BE IT ENACTED BY THE GENERAL ASSEMBLY OF THE STATE OF TENNESSEE:

SECTION 1. Notwithstanding any other provision of law to the contrary, the segment of Broad Street (U.S. Highways 11 and 72) in the City of Chattanooga from such street's intersection with West 32nd Street southward to its intersection with Tennessee Avenue (State Route 17), such segment including the WDEF studios at 3300 Broad Street, is hereby designated the "Luther Masingill Parkway" as a lasting tribute to an excellent broadcaster and public servant and even more accomplished human being.

SECTION 2. The Department of Transportation is directed to erect suitable signs or to affix suitable markers designating the segment of Broad Street described in Section 1 as the "Luther Masingill Parkway".

SECTION 3. The erection of such directional signs shall be within the guidelines prescribed by the *Manual on Uniform Traffic Control Devices*.

SECTION 4. This act shall become operative only if the federal highway administrator advises the Commissioner of Transportation in writing that the provisions of this act shall not render Tennessee in violation of federal laws and regulations and subject to penalties prescribed therein.

SECTION 5. This act shall become operative only if the cost of the manufacture and installation of such signs is paid to the Department of Transportation by the City of Chattanooga within one (1) year of the effective date of this act. Such payment shall be made prior to any expenditure by the state for the manufacture or installation of such signs. The department shall return any unused portion of the estimated cost to the City of Chattanooga within thirty (30) days of the erection of such signs. If the actual cost exceeds the estimated cost, an amount equal to the difference in such costs shall be remitted to the department by the City of Chattanooga within thirty (30) days of the county receiving an itemized invoice of the actual cost from the department.

SECTION 6. The appellation "Luther Masingill Parkway" provided for in this act is for honorary purposes only and nothing contained herein shall be construed as requiring the alteration of any address, or the governmental system for assigning addresses, in any county, municipality or other governmental entity affected by this act.

SECTION 7. Nothing contained in this act shall be construed as requiring the alteration of any previously named segment or segments of any highway described in this act as the "Luther Masingill Parkway".

SECTION 8. This act shall take effect upon becoming a law, the public welfare requiring it.

PASSED: April 15, 2010
Public Chapter No. 822 PUBLIC ACTS, 2010 3
APPROVED this 23rd day of April 2010

Photo by Holly Abernathy

James, Danny Howard (WDEF/WDOD/WUUQ Operations Manager), Luther, Bernie Barker (WDEF/WDOD/WUUQ General Manager) and Jeff Fontana (WDEF/WDOD/WUUQ General Sales Manager) on the day a portion of South Broad Street in Chattanooga became "Luther Masingill Parkway," August 2010.

Photo by Holly Abernathy

Luther with WDEF/WDOD/WUUQ General Manager Bernie Barker on the day a portion of South Broad Street became "Luther Masingill Parkway," August 2010.

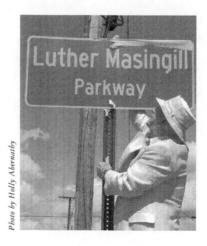

Photo by Holly Abernathy

Luther unveiling the sign for the portion of South Broad Street in Chattanooga named "Luther Masingill Parkway," August 2010.

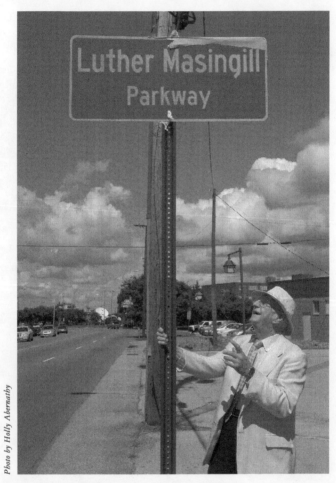

Luther after unveiling the sign for "Luther Masingill Parkway," August 2010.

Photo by Holly Abernathy

Luther and David Carroll on "Luther Masingill Parkway," August 2010.

Photo by Holly Abernathy

Luther and James on "Luther Masingill Parkway," August 2010.

———— ✥ ————

As shown in his response to having a street named after him, Luther is a very humble man. When I asked him about many of the awards and accolades he's received over the years as a broadcaster and a community servant, his responses were consistently humble. Luther has an unmatched career in broadcasting history. He has maintained the same time slot at the same station for over 70 years. It would take another volume to list the many accomplishments he has had over his more than 70 years in this industry.

I don't really follow the periodicals concerning broadcasting. I read them occasionally, Billboard *or some of the others that used to give you all the information like the station ratings. I never paid that much attention to them, but I kept informed. I read over the years about people who have been in the business a long time, how they got out of it or got into something else or have died. But no, I have not read about anybody being in it as long as I have. And yes, I was Young Man of the Year in 1953, awarded by the Jaycees, and that was an honor. Yes, Man of the Year. Just once. You can only get it once. You get it, you shut up, and you sit down. You take it and are appreciative of it. There's the Chattanoogan Man of the Year that I've received several times. It's a big thrill and people come up to you and say, "Hey! Congratulations, Luther!" and you're not quite sure what it's for or what they are talking about. "You're the Young Man of the Year," they say, or they tell you about some award you're up for or that they're about to name a part of a street after you. I'm just grateful. I really am.*

Image courtesy of WDEF-TV Archives

Congratulations, Luther

"Luther Masingill is a young man of exceptional character, of principle,
of devotion to God and to duty." Luther was named by the Jaycees as
Chattanooga's Young Man of the Year in 1953.

YOUNG MAN OF '53

The Jaycees have never honored a more popular Young Man of the Year than Luther Masingill, WDEF's voice about town. Luther, indeed, comes pretty close to being Chattanooga's man of the day every day along about getting-up time.

To many, many Chattanoogans, Luther exists only for the ear, visiting via radio. He's a gloom chaser at daybreak, a blues buster at breakfast, a carefree companion on the way to work. He's chatty, he's cheerful, he's a storehouse of information about things of importance at the moment, including such vital statistics as the state of the weather, whose dog is lost and what traffic conditions are.

But Luther Masingill is more than just a disembodied voice; he is a real force for good in the community, a servant of worthy causes who is as generous with himself and his talents as he is clever with his air time. His interests are varied, his contributions are many, his methods are effective.

Chattanooga is fortunate in having even one Luther Masingill at work in the civic, cultural and spiritual affairs of the city; it could use more like him. Perhaps it is just as well, though, that we have only one Luther Masingill on the air, since he is practically required listening.

We congratulate him on an honor well deserved; we commend the Jaycees on their choice of the year.

A column in the *Chattanooga Times* commends the Jaycees on their choice of Luther for Young Man of the Year in 1953: "He is a real force for good in the community, a servant of worthy causes who is as generous with himself and his talents as he is clever with his air time."

Photo courtesy of WDEF-TV Archives

Chattanooga Mayor Peter Rudolph "Rudy" Olgiati (second from the left) and
Tennessee Governor Frank G. Clement (third from the left) present Luther
with the Jaycees Young Man of the Year award in 1953.

Luther has received many awards over the course of his career. One unique honor was delivered on his 78th birthday by Congressman Zack Wamp on the floor of the United States House of Representatives. Here is the Congressional Record of what was spoken on Luther's birthday, March 9, 2000:

> Mr. Speaker, I rise today to honor a citizen who has contributed as much as anyone in the Third District of Tennessee to the wonderful quality of life that all of us who live there are privileged to enjoy. The occasion is his 78th birthday, but this tribute could be delivered any day. It is a testament to how universally known, loved and admired he is that you only have to say the word "Luther," and just about anyone will know you are referring to Luther Masingill, who has made Chattanooga's mornings brighter for 60 years.
>
> He signed on as host of his near universally known morning show on WDEF Radio, then an AM only station, on December 31, 1940. Franklin Delano Roosevelt was President then, and we were on the eve of World War II. Luther has seen Chattanooga-and the world-change mightily during his years on the air. Eleven U.S. Presidents as well as numerous Tennessee governors and Chattanooga mayors have come and gone while Luther has held way on the air. Luther has stayed on, however; and the "secrets" of his success and value to the Chattanooga area have remained the same.
>
> His radio show, now broadcast on WDEF AM and FM from 6-9 a.m. each weekday morning, does not focus on the controversies that tear us apart. By design, Luther devotes his show to the things that bring us together and make us human. Is your dog or cat missing? Would you like to buy or sell an animal? Is your civil club meeting or having a sale? His show is very much about neighbors helping neighbors and swapping information across the backyard fence, or at the grocery store, or after church. And his devoted listeners treat Luther as their friend and neighbor, which indeed he is.
>
> Luther plays relaxing, traditional music in between announcements; and his warm, reassuring voice has made countless folks in Southeast Tennessee, North Georgia, North Alabama and Western

North Carolina begin the day in a better spirit, no matter what the day may bring. He also does a spot on the noon news on Channel 12, WDEF Television, and he's been with that station since it signed on in 1954.

Today, March 9, 2000 is your 78th birthday, Luther; and so we say a loud "Happy Birthday!" and thanks for all you have done to enrich our lives and communities. And here's wishing you many more years on the air!

In addition to being mentioned on the floor of the House of Representatives during the 106th Congress, Luther has received many other honors during his career. For many years, I've called Luther, "Dr. Luther," because he has received various honorary doctorate degrees from some of the local colleges and universities. Some of these include honorary doctorates from Southern Missionary College, Tennessee Temple, and Southern University.

Image courtesy of WDEF-TV Archives

POST ESTABLISHED — The Luther Masingill Professorship in Communication at UTC was unveiled Tuesday.
Among those attending a reception were, from left, UTC Chancellor Dr. Frederick Obear; Mr. Masingill; Mrs. Masingill; and UTC communication department head Dr. Kit Rushing. (Staff photo by Scott Lee)

The UTC Luther Masingill Professorship in Communication was established in 1990 in honor of Luther's 50 years in broadcasting.

He is also an inaugural member of the Tennessee Radio Hall of Fame, into which I had the unique honor of inducting him in May 2012. Not only is Luther a veteran radio broadcaster, he is also a veteran television broadcaster. Luther was there when WDEF Television first signed on the air. He signed on the air with WDEF Radio on New Year's Eve in 1940 and signed on the air with WDEF-TV for the first time in 1954 on the 4th floor of the Volunteer Building.

Image courtesy of WDEF-TV Archives

LUTHER—Only member of the original WDEF staff of 1941 left is Luther Masingill. The city's 1953 Young Man of the Year says he had to clear his throat "10 times" when he read that first ad spot.

Luther at the WDEF-TV studios in 1954. He was there the first day WDEF-TV signed on the air, and present when WDEF Radio first signed on the air on New Year's Eve in 1940. Luther is the only remaining member of the original WDEF Radio staff of 1940-1941.

I was there at the television studio the very first day they went on the air. It was on a Sunday afternoon that they signed on. I was there and I've been there ever since. There were mainly speeches welcoming the television station to the city, and I think the camera panned around – the studios were just tiny then with very low ceilings – and they gave people a look because not many people had televisions then. People eventually started getting them, and within a short time, there were just hundreds and thousands of television sets, black and white of course, in the area. I was looking forward to that day when WDEF-TV signed on the air, but I knew there was more to television than there was radio, the mechanics of it. I remember going on the first program I was on and my time came to speak. I was so enthralled at what was going on in the studio – the people pointing and holding up this and pointing to that and all the cameras – that I missed my line completely. Somebody in back of me whispered, "It's your turn, Luther. It's your turn." So then I picked up the cue and read my line. From that moment on, I said, "Well, that's not too bad if I'll just pay attention and do what I'm supposed to do." As far as the salaries go, the first salary was very small, like the first salary of radio was very small, but we managed it. It was good being with those boys, like Jimmy Sampley, who was a photographer that we had, of course my friend Buddy Houts, and "Jolly Cholly" {Charles Krause}. There were just so many that came along over the years that we enjoyed working with and who contributed a lot to the success of the television and radio station.

Barbara Delanay Hofer, one of Luther's television co-hosts in those early days, recalls, "As a child growing up in Chattanooga, Tennessee, and as far back as I can remember, my family listened to Luther on the radio. It was in the late 1940s that I realized how important Luther was to our town. He kept his listeners abreast of everything that anyone needed to know to get through the day. It wasn't until 1951 that I was fortunate enough to meet Luther in person. While in my second year of college at the University of Tennessee at Chattanooga, I was studying flute and learned of an opening for second flute in the Chattanooga Symphony. I was invited to the audition and won the position. One evening the symphony was traveling to Nashville to perform, and on the program was *Peter and the Wolf* by Prokofiev, a narrative piece for children. Luther was to be the guest narrator, and we sat together and chatted on the bus on the way up to Nashville. That evening Luther's narration was a huge hit. In all my experience over the years, as well as becoming principal flutist in the Savannah Symphony Orchestra, Luther's performance of *Peter and the Wolf* that evening was the best and most perfect I have ever heard. A few years later when the first television station, WDEF, went on the air in Chattanooga, "The Luther Show" needed a sidekick. I was also working in radio as a talk show host at WAPO and was still playing in the symphony. One day I got a call from Hap Anderson, who introduced himself as the manager of the new WDEF Television station. He said he wanted to know if I would be interested in auditioning to be Luther Masingill's co-host on his program, "The Luther Show." I attempted to remain dignified, but when I hung up, I let out a happy scream. When audition day came and Luther walked into the studio, he smiled and hugged me and we began to talk just as we did years ago. I got the job, along with co-hosting a 'Top Ten Dance Party' with WDEF announcers Pete Griffin and Neil Miller, which aired at noon on Saturdays. We had fun over the years. Luther, Buddy Houts and I would sometimes leave the fourth floor of the old Volunteer Building where the studios were located and go across the street to Woolworth's for an afternoon treat. Buddy could always make you laugh. He was one of Luther's best friends and his mentor. I eventually left WDEF-TV due to my husband's career change that eventually led us to Savannah, Georgia, but I can say that Luther has stayed the same. He has always loved his work and has cared about the needs of others and of his audience."

Luther with his very first WDEF-TV co-host Barbara Delaney Hofer
in the late 1950s.

Luther and co-host Barbara Delaney Hofer in the late 1950s.

Photo courtesy of WDEF-TV Archives

Luther on the set of a WDEF-TV commercial in the 1950s. The camera seen here is one of the first cameras WDEF-TV acquired.

Photo courtesy of WDEF-TV Archives

Luther during a guest interview in the early days on **WDEF-TV**.

Photo courtesy of WDEF-TV Archives

Luther on the set of a **WDEF-TV** commercial for Bardahl Motor Oil
in the early 1960s.

NOPE, GUESS AGAIN!—This is not a be-wigged Luther Masingill, beating the drums for the cause of metro. It's Ringo Starr, percussion man for the Beatles, the sensational British rock 'n' roll group, who will be seen in full concert on closed-circuit television screen this Saturday and Sunday at Memorial Auditorium. Show times are 12 noon and 2:30 p.m. Saturday; 2:30 p.m. Sunday. The show is the Beatles' debut performance at Washington, and with them are Lesley Gore and the Beach Boys.

Luther was often kidded about how he resembled Beatles drummer Ringo Starr, only without the hair.

Luther during a voice-over in 1958.

LUTHER'S DAY OF SLAVERY—They gave Luther Masingill away as a bonus "prize" at Engel Stadium Tuesday night, the lucky lady having the effervescent radio man's services as yard boy for today. Photo shows Luther "slaving" with a power mower on the spacious lawn of Mrs. Harold Kenslow of 1901 Airport Road, who "won" the mike man. Mrs. Kenslow, who is a clerk at Blue Cross-Blue Shield offices here, directs Luther's labors, while her grandfather, William Grandon, chaperons the visit of the pride of WDEF.—(Staff Photo by Jim Mooney.)

Luther "slaving" after being given away as a bonus prize at Engel Stadium the previous Tuesday evening. Once lucky lady was given "the pride of WDEF" and his services as "yard boy" for the day.

Photo courtesy of WDEF-TV Archives

Luther on the set of a WDEF-TV commercial.

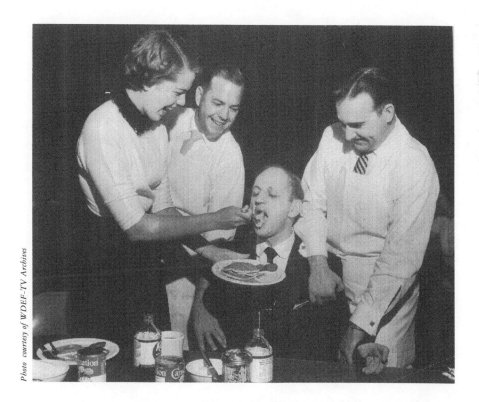

Photo courtesy of WDEF-TV Archives

Luther during a pancake-cooking segment on **WDEF-TV** in the early 1960s.

Photo courtesy of WDEF-TV Archives

Luther during a live TV commercial on WDEF-TV for a local appliance store.

Photo courtesy of WDEF-TV Archives

Luther with American conductor and composer Leonard Bernstein of the New York Philharmonic.

Luther with Leonard Bernstein of the New York Philharmonic.

Photo courtesy of WDEF-TV Archives

Luther and TV weatherman "Big Jim" Hill.

Photo courtesy of WDEF-TV Archives

Luther receiving a "parking ticket" in the late 1950s.

Photo courtesy of WDEF-TV Archives

Luther with Ernie Fagan during a station promotion. They made a bet
and Luther won, so Ernie had to push him through the crowd. During the
stunt, Luther turns his face just as the horse decides to relieve himself during
the procession.

Photo courtesy of WDEF-TV Archives

Luther striping the road during a station promotion.

Photo courtesy of WDEF-TV Archives

Luther and his Model T along with co-host, Barbara Delaney Hofer and her 1929 Packard on Patten Parkway in Chattanooga. Luther's 1923 Model T is on display at the Towing and Recovery Museum on South Broad Street in Chattanooga.

Luther with the employees of the Tennessee Valley Railroad Museum
during a live remote broadcast.

Photo courtesy of WDEF-TV Archives

Luther standing in front of his Model T with Bob Harrington, known as the "Chaplain of Bourbon Street," from New Orleans, and Forest Cate, the son of the owner of the Ford dealership in Chattanooga.

Photo courtesy of WDEF-TV Archives

Luther with friend and coworker Warren Herring in the early 1970s.

Luther with Jerry Lingerfelt (then station manager of WDEF Radio) and server Louise at a local restaurant, August 1970.

Image courtesy of WDEF-TV Archives

From left, three of the original WDEF-TV crew members, Emroy "Willie" Williamson, Luther Masingill and Peyton Brien. (Staff photo by Mike O'Neal)

Luther with two of the other original WDEF-TV crew members, Emory "Willie" Williamson and Peyton Brien, September 24, 1989.

Photo courtesy of WDEF-TV Archives

Luther with Patrick Core and Linda Edwards in the 1990s.

Photo by Holly Abernathy

Luther standing outside of the Volunteer Building where his career began many years ago, September 2010.

4

Luther the Husband and Father

Luther's broadcasting career continued to progress, and his personal life was moving forward as well. Luther was closer to meeting the woman he would spend the rest of his life with, Mary Varnell. Luther and Mary's marriage has always inspired me. When I asked him how long he had been married, he pulled off his ring to look at the inscription, "M.F.V. to W.L.M. 4-27-1957". He has given me advice over the years, and I have been a student of his marriage. Anyone that has been married for any length of time knows there are challenges that come along with any marriage. To see one that has survived for so long and with so much love, respect, and admiration for each other has challenged and inspired me in my own marriage to my wife, Christy.

I asked both Luther and Mary how they met. Was it love at first sight? Were there sparks and stars in their eyes when they met? Well, sort of, but not in the way you might think. After Luther and Mary met, their relationship eventually evolved from friendship into love.

When I met my first and only wife, Mary, it was in church in the hallway when I ran into her. I actually ran right into her. I bumped into her at the corner of the hallway in our church and that was it. I looked at her and I thought, "Gee whiz! Wow!" I was impressed. I liked her looks. I liked her voice. She did not bless me out for running into her. She just said, "Oh, I'm sorry," in a very soft voice that just captivated me. That was my first encounter, and from that moment on, I was entranced.

From the personal collection of Luther and Mary Masingill

Luther and Mary share a rare private moment on their wedding day,
April 27, 1957.

From the personal collection of Luther and Mary Masingill

Luther and Mary on their wedding day, April 27, 1957.

I was very much impressed and I thought she would make a good wife for somebody and I thought, "Ma'am, I'd like to be included in that!" So later on we became married.

I often like to tease Luther because he was once named Bachelor of the Year. He said he, of course, liked to date different girls when he had the time, but that once he met Mary, that was pretty much it for him.

Yes, Mr. Bachelor. I think that came out one time. Yes, I was 83 then {laughs}. No, I was in my 30s or something like that and someone wanted to know if I was married. When they found out I wasn't, they said, "Let's make him the Bachelor of the Year." I received that honor, if it's an honor, at one time, yes. I liked dating different girls, but when you meet one that you really are impressed with, you kind of concentrate on that. At the time, since my father died, I had the responsibility of kind of taking care of my younger brother and my younger sister and my mother. There just wasn't a lot of time to date and spend time with girls, but I did find time to be with Mary and to grow in friendship and eventually love. When I did finally ask her to marry me, she said NO! {Laughs} No, she said yes.

When I asked Mary about her first meeting with Luther, she admitted that she had no idea he was on the radio or television. She really had no idea who Luther was or what he did for a living: "When I first met him, I did not recall ever seeing him anywhere or someone introducing us. I was in my senior year of high school at the time, and of course, we both went to the same church, Avondale Baptist Church in East Chattanooga. I took a job as a secretary at the church, and when I started working there, Luther's mother, her name is also Mary, and I became really good friends. We just had a great time at the church, although I was supposed to be working and she was there doing volunteer work. But we just really became fast friends, and I don't know, I suppose she must have mentioned me to Luther or something because all of the sudden he was there at the church in the afternoons. I noticed that he just kept coming over, and every time I would look up, there he would be. He would just say, 'I'm Luther. My mom comes over and does some volunteer work,' and I would say, 'Oh, Okay.'

At the time, I did not know Luther from the proverbial house cat. He was just somebody that was hanging around the church. I did not know him as radio Luther or anything like that. I'd never even heard of him. I think he started his radio career in 1940 or '41 and I was still just a baby then. He always tells all those awful jokes and I tell him, 'You quit telling those jokes on me,' but he is 14 years older than I am. I don't know if he felt like he had to raise me or not, but I was of legal age when we married. He waited until I was 21. But in the beginning, he just kept coming over to the church and we would just talk. Finally one night after church, he went to my parents and asked if he could take me home from church and stop to get a Coke. I don't really know if they knew who he was or that he was the man on the radio. I think they did, but at that time in his career, he was just a radio announcer. That was back in 1952 or '53, somewhere around there, but he took me home that night after church and after that he started taking me out more often.

The friendship just evolved as time went on, and I realized that Luther was a really nice guy, somebody that I could trust. I felt he had picked me out, coming over to the church all the time like he did. Probably the thing that struck me the most was that he was kind and he was gentle – and funny and cute. Eventually Luther started letting me borrow his car [*laughs*]. But it's not like in the movies or anything. It's not like a great awakening where I realize this man is in love with me. It was just something that evolved. Soon after I graduated from high school, I went out to St. Louis, Missouri, to airline school. When I finished, I was 21 and that was when I came back home and we started dating seriously. And as I said, I knew his mother, and besides his mother, one of his sisters became a really good friend of mine. So it was just kind of like a family thing that more or less evolved. Of course his family lived about two houses down from the church, so he has always been interested in the church and doing the work and volunteering his time there too. But that was our 'meeting' if you want to describe it that way."

Luther often likes to tease Mary, and as Mary mentioned, to make jokes about the age difference between them. He often jokes that, when they got married, he went on the honeymoon and Mary went off to summer camp to ride horses and go canoeing. When you see Luther and Mary together, you can see the deep love they have for one another, and you can see the comfort and familiarity of having been together for more than 55 years. It's a beautiful thing and something I aspire to have in my own life with my wife.

I was 32 years old when we got married. We had dated for a while. I tried to kiss her on the first date, but she wouldn't let me. On the second date, though, she did let me. But I remember asking her to marry me. I was parked up on Missionary Ridge, what is now the cut in the ridge. We were just parked up there, looking at the lights of the city, and that's when I asked her to marry me. She said, "Okay, I'll marry you." So yes, we met in church and started dating, and we set a wedding date and got married and it's been hell ever since {laughs}. No, I'm just kidding. It's been a good marriage and I am thankful that I married Mary.

From the personal collection of Luther and Mary Masingill

Miss Varnell, Mr. Masingill To Wed April 27

Miss Mary Frances Varnell, daughter of Mr. and Mrs. Joseph K. Varnell, has chosen Saturday, April 27, as the date of her marriage to William Luther Masingill. The prospective bridegroom is the son of Mrs. Mary H. Masingill and the late W. T. Masingill.

The wedding will take place at the Avondale Baptist Church at 2 o'clock in the afternoon. The Rev. L. R. Whidden will officiate at the ceremony and a program of nuptial music will be presented by Manning Sullivan.

Miss Varnell will be given in marriage by her father. Mrs. B. E. Weathington will serve as matron of honor and bridesmaids will be Mrs. David Reynolds and Mrs. Clay Johnson.

Tom Masingill will attend his brother as best man. Ushers will be Jim Hill, Charles Masingill, brother of Mr. Masingill, Warren Herring and David Reynolds.

Wedding Plans Announced

"Wedding Plans Announced" in the March 28, 1957 edition of the *Chattanooga News-Free Press* for Miss Mary Frances Varnell and William Luther Masingill.

When Mary completed her schooling, she was offered a job in Chicago but could not imagine leaving Chattanooga. When I asked Mary about that decision she made as a young woman, she reflected on her life with Luther: "It's been wonderful with Luther. I could not think of how I could have lived a better 55 years. It would certainly have been dull without him, and of course, we have our two children now and our grandchildren. The years have gone by in what seems like such a fast pace. You separate it into the time when there was just the two of us and then when we started having our children. Then you have the children and you are so busy with them and taking care of their needs and doing things at home. Thank goodness I was a stay-at-home mom when the children were smaller. In my mind, I have divided it up into sections of our lives. It has just been wonderful, and each era that we have gone through has just been better than the last. It's just been a great 55 years that he has been with me. I just thank the Lord every day that I have him for another day. Our time together has just been wonderful, our little vacations that we take the kids on, the beach. Sometimes you just sit back and you think of all those things way back and how we've really had some great times together."

From the personal collection of Luther and Mary Masingill

Luther's wife-to-be, Mary Frances Varnell, featured in the
January 11, 1957, edition of *The Lookout*.

From the personal collection of Luther and Mary Masingill

Luther and Mary sign their marriage certificate.

From the personal collection of Luther and Mary Masingill

—Ed Forstner Studio.

MRS. WILLIAM LUTHER MASINGILL

Miss Mary Frances Varnell Says
Her Vows With Luther Masingill

The announcement in the Sunday, April 28, 1957, edition of the *Chattanooga Times* that the marriage of Miss Mary Frances Varnell and Luther Masingill had taken place the previous day.

From the personal collection of Luther and Mary Masingill

The entire wedding party on the day of Luther and Mary's wedding.

Luther jokingly makes faces at a police officer on his wedding day.

Luther and Mary on their wedding day, April 27, 1957.

From the personal collection of Luther and Mary Masingill

Luther and Mary pose for a kiss in front of the cameras on their wedding day,
April 27, 1957.

From the personal collection of Luther and Mary Masingill

Luther and Mary's wedding reception at the house where they still live today.

From the personal collection of Luther and Mary Masingill

Luther and Mary at the Chattanooga Airport as they remove all the "gags" after their wedding.

From the personal collection of Luther and Mary Masingill

Luther and Mary underneath the wing of the airplane before leaving on their honeymoon in the Bahamas.

From the personal collection of Luther and Mary Masingill

Luther and Mary smile for the cameras as they board the plane on their way to their honeymoon in the Bahamas.

Luther and Mary are "Just Married" on April 27, 1957.

The British Colonial Hotel
NASSAU, BAHAMAS

Luther and Mary stayed at The British Colonial Hotel on their honeymoon.

Luther and Mary during their honeymoon in the Bahamas.

From the personal collection of Luther and Mary Masingill

Luther and Mary, April 1959.

From the personal collection of Luther and Mary Masingill

Luther and Mary, late 1970s.

From the personal collection of Luther and Mary Masingill

Luther and Mary, poolside, at the home of their dear friend
Buddy Houts, 1981.

From the personal collection of Luther and Mary Masingill

Luther and Mary, 1965.

Luther and Mary, early 1970s.

Luther and Mary, early 1970s.

Luther and Mary, June 1977.

Luther and Mary on Lake Superior in October 1991.

When I think about the moments in my life that have brought total joy and happiness, I've got to say that two of those moments were when my daughters were born. I've always wanted two girls. My wife, Christy, has epilepsy and the birth of our first daughter, Gracie, was quite an adventure.

Gracie came suddenly. The baby was breech, and with my wife's epilepsy, we had to rush to the hospital with Life Force on standby. With my other daughter, Lucy, we did not even know Christy was pregnant until she was well into her second trimester. Before Lucy came along, I really wanted a second child. I remember many mornings at work sharing with Luther, as coworkers often do, my desire to have another child. When we did find out that Christy was pregnant that second time, I said, "Luther, it's a girl and she is going to be here in less than three

Photo courtesy of James Howard

Christy with daughter, Gracie, in 1994.

months! Can you believe it?" He just stood there and said, "What?" For weeks Luther would come into the studio and ask me if I was kidding. When Lucy did come into this world a few months later, Luther was on vacation. He was in Texas that week visiting with his family, so he was not on the air that day. In the emergency room where Lucy was delivered, they had Sunny 92.3 WDEF playing on the radio. So after they cleaned Lucy up and had her all swaddled and I was holding her, the first phone call I made was to the studio. David Carroll was filling in for Luther that day and he put me live on the air. So everyone in Chattanooga who was listening to Sunny 92.3 knew about Lucy before the family. They knew what she looked like, how long she was and how much she weighed. My wife, Christy, couldn't believe I'd done that. While the family is waiting in the hallway, I was describing my daughter to the rest of Chattanooga! It was an exciting time.

Photo courtesy of James Howard

James flying an airplane with daughter, Lucy, in 2011.

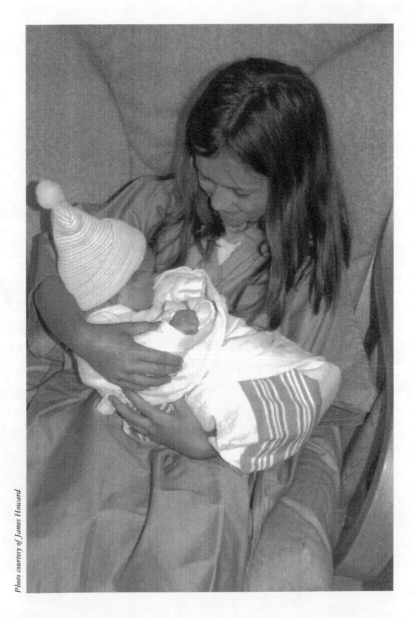

Photo courtesy of James Howard

James' daughters, Gracie and Lucy, in July 2008 just after Lucy was born.

When it comes to my girls, Luther loves Lucy and Gracie. Luther and Lucy have a special connection that is indescribable. He loves both girls, but there is a special connection between Luther and Lucy. When Lucy was younger, she had some trouble with her vocabulary. Despite the trouble with her speech, she would point to a photograph I have of Luther and me and say, "Lutha." That was one of the first words out of her mouth. Along with my girls, children have a way of grabbing at Luther's heart. Luther seldom gets teary-eyed or emotional, but children have that effect on him. He has a compassionate heart when it comes to children.

The smile of a child is a most disarming thing. It's just the smile, the way they react to you. Sometimes at church, a momma will come in holding her child, and I'll go up and ask them how they're doing and they just start smiling. I love the warmness and the smile of a child. It's the greatest thing in the world.

I share Luther's compassion for children and family. Over the years, I have been able to glean little pieces of advice from Luther, simple things he has given me. For example, I will tell him about projects or events in which I am involved and he will tell me, "Well, that sounds fun, but listen, don't sacrifice your family." When I am in my 70s and 80s, I too will probably look back and think I should have spent more time with my family. I don't want to have too many regrets in life, none of us do. I look at Luther and I know he is not a perfect man, but I respect his advice and what he has learned over the years. The advice he has given me regarding family is: "Put your family first. Don't have any regrets."

Luther and Mary were married on April 27, 1957, and they were blessed with their children shortly thereafter. Luther talks about his kids all the time, but I've often wondered what the dynamic was like when they were just a young family. I was 19 years old when I met Luther for the first time. When I started working at WDEF in 1993, I knew about Luther's children, Jeffrey and Joanie. I had heard about his wife, Mary, and Luther's family life through the radio but working with him allowed me to put some of the pieces together. It allowed me to see the value he puts on the lives of his children and on them being happy and healthy. He told me when both of my girls were born that there is nothing like the feeling when you are holding your child for the first time and you look at their face and you know they have a good set of lungs. Their health is a gift and you thank God for it. Luther experienced this awe twice with the birth of his own children and describes what that meant to him. He also reflected back on his own upbringing and how he did not change very much when his two kids came along.

Things weren't that different with my own kids. I did not change too much. My parents were fairly strict parents, both of them, and of course they insisted that we go to school and we did. They insisted we go to church and we did. All of us had little jobs to do around the house, and Daddy saw to it that we did them. There wasn't too much difference, and I felt the same way about Jeffrey and Joanie as they came along in our marriage. In fact Jeffrey would ask, "Daddy is there anything I can do? You want me to cut the grass?" Joanie would help Mary in the kitchen. We had a good family and a good family

From the personal collection of Luther and Mary Masingill

Luther with his children, Jeffrey and Joanie, November 1960.

relationship. Jeffrey wasn't that crazy about school, but he did complete it and everything turned out fine. But there really is something special about the birth of your children.

Jeffrey came first. He was a Mother's Day present, I guess you might say. He was born on Mother's Day at Memorial Hospital and I was there. Mary was there of course and it was an exciting morning – a Sunday morning. We knew it was going to be a boy, and we were just so happy. It was just a great day. We were so thankful. When you're old enough and you have sense enough, you are so thankful that the child is all right. Jeffrey did not have any hair at first {laughs}, but we were so glad the child was healthy. That's what is most important and you thank the Lord for it that day.

A short time later, Joanie came along. There's a couple of years difference between them. Of course, back in those days you weren't invited into the delivery room, but it was just an average birth and she was such a beautiful child. We were so thankful. She had all the fingers and all the toes, and she was a beautiful child and she still is. Now that she's married, she's presented us with a couple of great grandchildren, two boys. She's been married over 25 years I guess. In fact, I made the last payment on her wedding just last week {laughs}. Yeah, I sure did.

From the personal collection of Luther and Mary Masingill

Luther's daughter, Joanie, November 1960.

The Masingill family, May 1961.

Luther and Mary's children, Jeffrey and Joanie, in the mid 1970s.

From the personal collection of Luther and Mary Masingill

Luther's daughter, Joan Masingill Brown, with her husband, Mike, and sons, Evan and Ian, in the mid 1990s.

From the personal collection of Luther and Mary Masingill

Luther with his daughter, Joanie, in Malaysia in 2000.

Luther's wife Mary says they were just a normal family just like any other. She describes Luther as a loving father. "He was a great dad. He was not terribly involved with the kids in sporting activities, but he was always there for them. When they were little, he would get them ready for bed and read stories to them. We have a lot of photos where he really enjoyed reading to them. He was great with the kids. They love him."

From the personal collection of Luther and Mary Masingill

Luther reading to his son Jeffrey, May 1960.

From the personal collection of Luther and Mary Masingill

Luther and his son Jeffrey repair a chair together, May 1961.

Mary also described what it was like around the holidays when the children were young. "One thing I remember in particular is that when it was Christmas time, Luther would have to work if Christmas day fell on a weekday. So the kids would not want to come in to where the Christmas tree was and where Santa had left the toys until Daddy got home from work. They always waited until he got home in the morning, which was usually around 10:00 or 10:30 at that time. They were anxious and I would tell him to hurry because it was hard to keep two kids at the back of the house while the front is full of toys. But they love their dad. Some of our best memories are the day-to-day things you do with your children.

You help them with their homework, make sure that they are choosing the right friends and making the right decisions. I remember when Joanie was in school and they had a special day for the fathers. She was to put together a picnic basket and go on a picnic with her dad. So he took her on a special father-daughter picnic. It was just small things like that that they remember with their dad. At that time he was doing radio in the morning from 6:00 a.m. to 10:00 a.m., and then he was also doing afternoons. By the time he got home at 4:00 p.m. or so in the afternoon, he was pretty tired, but the kids were really rambunctious. They would give him time to take a little short nap, and then they would be up and playing again, but our routines were pretty average. Even though he was well known by a lot of people, we were just a quiet, normal family, living in the same house that we bought when we got married."

During a recent interview, Luther described what life was like when his children were younger:

No matter how tired you are, when you have a child and you are enamored with that child, you try to get hold of it as soon as you get home from work. You hold it and then when it needs changing you hand it over to her {laughs}. No, I helped change the babies. I loved holding Jeffrey and Joanie. I'd lay back on the couch and they would fall asleep. They'd fall asleep on my tummy. Then in later years, they knew that daddy, because he got up at 4:15 in the morning, would probably take a nap sometime during the afternoon. If they planned something, they'd have to plan it either before or after my nap, and then I would run them wherever they wanted to go.

We did a lot of things over the years. We never did go to Disney World, but we did go to things like Six Flags Over Georgia in Atlanta. I remember one time we stopped in North Carolina at a town that had a roller coaster. The kids wanted to ride, but they were too small then; they weren't tall enough. So they wanted us to go ahead, so they could watch Mary and I ride. So we got on, and I remember starting up that long, winding thing and looking down, and there they are, two tiny little people looking up at their momma and daddy and hoping their momma and daddy were going to get back okay {laughs}. They've been two lovely children and they've turned out just great and I'm grateful for them. And you always thank the Lord for sending them to you.

I asked Jeffery Masingill about what it was like growing up as Luther's son. He replied: "It seemed like there was always family around. There were cousins and aunts and uncles around all the time. Mom and Dad both

From the personal collection of Luther and Mary Masingill

The Masingill family (left to right): Mary, Jeffrey, Joan and Luther, October 1962.

came from large families, lots of brothers and sisters, so there were always cousins around. There was always family at the house and we were always doing something as kids, playing and just having a good time. We were not rich, by any means, but we were comfortable. Dad took care of us. We always had everything we needed, such as food on the table and that kind of thing. Anytime he had a vacation, we would always go somewhere. I remember going to Florida, Fort Sumter, Washington, D.C., and places like that. We would be gone for a week and go somewhere and have a great time. The church was also very important to my dad. If he wasn't at work at the radio station, many times he was at the church fixing things – fixing a door, changing lights or anything that needed to be done. I would go up to the church with him and help him paint something or just whatever needed to be done to help maintain the church over in Avondale. We spent a lot of time together over the years just doing things like that together."

Luther's daughter, Joanie, remembers her childhood filled with family as well: "There was always family over at our house. Like my Uncle Tom – they were always overseas somewhere – so when Uncle Tom would come back to the States with his family, they would come and stay with us. And I remember our little house so many times just being filled with people and cooking hamburgers and sitting outside, just those kinds of memories, of family, of just having a family."

It's a miracle that they are born. When they come into this world and you look at your own, Jeffrey and Joanie – and I was at the birth of her first child out in Texas – so yes, to me it's a miracle. I don't know how else to describe it. If you're religious and you pray that the child is going to be okay and it is, you're grateful and you thank God for it, for that gift of a newborn child coming into the world. It just makes you feel good when you see them. And then as time passes, your children have children. They call out to you, "Hey Papaw, you want to help me with…?" I love that Papaw deal; it's a good feeling. And you send them Christmas cards and you slip a few bucks in it where they can enjoy something they want to get for themselves. It's just great to get to do things for them as they grow up and to see them grow and watch them care for each other.

I have grown to cherish Saturday and Sunday mornings with my daughters, Gracie and Lucy. I cook breakfast for them, and I get to have my morning time with them. I'm not there with Christy in the early hours during the week, getting them ready for school and sharing in all the responsibilities of the day's beginning. Because of this, I cherish my time with them on Saturday and Sunday mornings even more. Luther's daughter, Joanie, can relate to what it was like having her dad gone in the mornings while he was on the radio: "It was great. I mean we never had breakfast together or anything like that because we were sitting at the table listening to him. We had breakfast with him in a different way. There is security there because you are listening to him and you know where he is."

Even though Luther wasn't home for breakfast in the mornings, there were some perks to being one of Luther's kids. They were aware that he was a well-known personality early on.

Jeffrey and Joanie picked up on the fact that I was on the radio and TV very quickly. In fact, Joanie would offer to come down on snowy days to answer the phone, take messages, list the schools that were closed due to the snow and just whatever else she could do. She loved the business and it always tickled her when we would be out somewhere, eating or shopping, and somebody would say, "Hey Luther! I heard you on the radio this morning! That's Joanie, right?" or "That's Jeffrey, right?" It tickled them to have that recognition.

Joanie liked knowing the day before that they were going to close the schools due to snow. "That was always a nice little perk," she says. "When it did snow, sometimes I would go down with Daddy to the old studio down on Broad Street. One snow day, I had gone down with him and answered phones all morning, one call after the next. There were a number of cancellations and the calls just kept coming in. It was just so much fun. I remember at the very end someone came in and handed me a check for five dollars. I thought that was the greatest thing in the world that I had made five dollars! I don't remember how old I was; I must have been maybe 10 or 11. But it was a fun morning, and I enjoyed talking to people as they were calling in because they knew Dad; they recognized him. It was also funny because they would just keep talking to me and say things like, "Oh, I remember the day you were born." I still remember those days down at the station answering the phones and seeing Daddy work. There was also the fascination of when they were still playing records. I loved seeing my dad on one side of the glass and the other guy being on the other side of the glass. It was just a really neat time that I'll always remember."

When you're in the broadcasting business, the hours required are not at all traditional. As a morning show co-host, I get up at 2:30 in the morning, and sometimes I miss out on special moments with my wife and kids, as many broadcasters do. The life of a broadcasting professional has many challenges that most people never see. Many only see or hear what is on the radio or television and think that is where the job ends for the day. In contrast to general perception, the work done on the air is only a small portion of a broadcaster's job. The hours are long and the requirements, such as production, research and show preparation, can be quite challenging and are much more than most people understand. Mary Masingill describes taking on that challenge when she and Luther first got married: "Four o'clock in the morning? I will tell you, when we first got married, we came back from our honeymoon and got settled into the house and Luther was ready to go back to work. The first morning that he went back to work after our honeymoon, I got up at 4:00 a.m. and I fixed breakfast. I mean we had bacon and eggs, toast and jelly, coffee and everything, and we both just sat there and looked at it. Neither one of us ate a bit of it, and he says, 'Honey, forget breakfast.' So now our morning routine is: I am still in bed asleep and he gets up and gets ready to go to work. He comes in and kisses me goodbye and he says, 'I'll see you after while,' and I say, 'Okay.' That is our morning routine and it has been for many years. Of course it varied a little bit when the kids were in school but not much. I can remember once or twice in the 55 years we've been married when he has had the flu or something, but he never gets sick. So that has been our routine since we've been married. He would get up and leave the house early in the morning, and then around 9:00 or 9:30 a.m., he would call me and we would talk for a little while. Those are our mornings together."

Luther and Mary were able to find a sense of normalcy within the demanding hours that he worked, but the holidays could be just as challenging. The hours worked by a broadcaster are long and varied, and holidays are not always ideal in the life of a broadcaster. Those who have ever had a job in this industry have undoubtedly worked on a holiday. It's expected, especially if you are just getting started in your career. Luther's son Jeffrey describes growing up with a father in broadcasting and what it was like when Luther had to work on Christmas day. "My dad was always making home movies, back in the 16-millimeter film days when we were kids. He would act like Cecil B. DeMille or a lot of the great directors at the time. He would say, 'Go do this' and 'You, stand behind the door and come in,' and he was always directing us as he was shooting films [*laughs*]. We would have to wait for our cue to come in, especially on Christmas morning. If Christmas came on a weekday, he was working, so we had to wait until after 10 o'clock in the morning when he got home to have our Christmas. Of course we were awake at dawn waiting for dad to come home, waiting to see what Santa Claus brought us for Christmas. Then when he did get home, we would have to pretend we were asleep so he could film us going in.

Joanie says she has many memories, too, of knowing that all the things were sitting in the living room under the Christmas tree and they couldn't go in to see them: "I did not want to peek because I did not want to spoil the surprise, but we would spend time back in Mom and Dad's bedroom and watch their little tiny black-and-white TV until Dad got home. Once he got home, he had to get his movie camera all set up and ready to go so that he could choreograph and stage everything [*laughs*]. It was so exciting to us if Christmas fell on a Saturday or Sunday, but we still had to wait until he got the camera!"

Of course I worked on Christmas.... A lot of Christmases I worked and they'd have to wait until I came home to open the gifts. They did not want to open the gifts until Daddy got there on Christmas morning. They got used to it, I think, and they just made the best of it. They had breakfast and did not go into that room where the gifts were until Daddy arrived and then we all went in together. I did not – and still do not – put too much importance in gifts and things, but we always saw that the children received what they wanted for Christmas if it was within reason. It was the same way for Mary. And she in turn remembered me at Christmas time. It was just a time of sweet expression in addition to being a religious time of the year. I love the real meaning of Christmas.

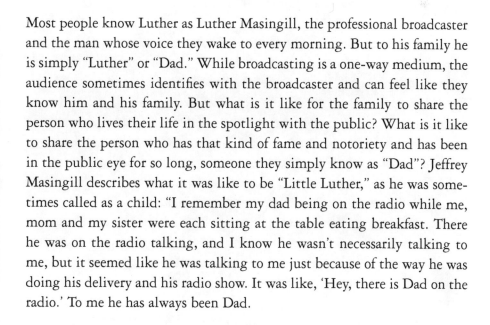

Most people know Luther as Luther Masingill, the professional broadcaster and the man whose voice they wake to every morning. But to his family he is simply "Luther" or "Dad." While broadcasting is a one-way medium, the audience sometimes identifies with the broadcaster and can feel like they know him and his family. But what is it like for the family to share the person who lives their life in the spotlight with the public? What is it like to share the person who has that kind of fame and notoriety and has been in the public eye for so long, someone they simply know as "Dad"? Jeffrey Masingill describes what it was like to be "Little Luther," as he was sometimes called as a child: "I remember my dad being on the radio while me, mom and my sister were each sitting at the table eating breakfast. There he was on the radio talking, and I know he wasn't necessarily talking to me, but it seemed like he was talking to me just because of the way he was doing his delivery and his radio show. It was like, 'Hey, there is Dad on the radio.' To me he has always been Dad.

Luther and his son Jeffrey, January 1973.

I know he is 'Luther,' but I just looked at him more as dad and not as this celebrity. I knew he was a celebrity, and of course every time I got to school, everybody reminded me of that fact by calling me, 'Little Luther.' I got it all through school. It was flattering being called that, but after a few years, it got a little old. No offense to Dad, but my name is Jeff. He did not name me Luther Junior, but that is who I was all through school, 'Little Luther' and 'Luther Junior.'

I would watch him as he would work, as he would talk and go through his papers. Then his engineer would point at him and say, 'Okay, you're on the air, go!' Then he would start talking and I would be sitting in the back in the corner watching him, thinking how cool it was to see all this. To me he was 'Luther,' yes, but he was 'Dad' and there I was sitting watching my dad do his job. I wasn't really seeing him as Luther on the radio, because to me he was just dad doing his job. He was on the radio, and it was just fascinating to sit there and watch him do it. I just remember how it seemed that everybody tuned in to hear Luther. Before you had the morning shows, he was the main place to go as far as information and what was happening with schools and the city. This was especially true when it snowed around here, which was rare, but Luther is where people got their information. I remember thinking back then, maybe the first or second time I had gone down to the station with him, that I wanted to be in radio and in broadcasting. As a kid, this was what I wanted to do – just going and seeing everything and hearing him on the radio and then being able to go down there and be in the studio and see where he actually worked. It fascinated me. Sometimes as a kid you want to be a fireman or a policeman, but the first couple of times I went down to the station with dad, I knew this is what I wanted to do. I thought, 'Gee, I want to do this when I grow up.' Maybe it was like Dale Earnhardt Jr., looking at his dad all the time and wanting to grow up and become a racecar driver. I wanted to be Dad. I wanted to be on the radio. It was fascinating to me at that time."

From the personal collection of Luther and Mary Masingill

Luther and Jeffrey, October 1958.

From the personal collection of Luther and Mary Masingill

Mary, Jeffrey, and Luther on Jeffrey's second birthday, May 1960.

From the personal collection of Luther and Mary Masingill

The Masingill family, December 1968.

Luther's son Jeffrey, May 2009.

I have often wondered if Luther's kids received any special treatment, especially with the title that Jeffrey had of "Luther Junior." I know I had an experience or two when the mention of Luther's name got me out of trouble. One such instance was in my early days of radio when I was doing the air shift after Luther. He went off the air at 9:00 a.m. and I started at 9:00 a.m. This particular morning I had overslept, which was rare for me. In order to get to work on time, I was speeding, and a police officer pulled me over. Rain was pouring down that morning, and I had already pulled over on the side of the road before he turned his lights on. I knew he was going to bust me because he had done a u-turn. I had my license out and actually ran to his patrol car waving it (which is a good way to get shot!). I blurted out, "I work with Luther and he is going to be mad at me if I get there late!" It was kind of funny, but he said, "Mr. Howard, I don't want to catch you speeding again on my roads. Tell Luther I said hi."

Joanie had a similar experience many years ago: "I was driving to work one Saturday morning, going down Brainerd Road toward East Gate Mall to go to my job at Loveman's. I was married and on my license it says 'Joan Masingill Brown.' I got pulled over for something – I cannot remember exactly what – and the officer looked at my license. He said, 'Oh, are you Luther's daughter?' I told him I was and he said, 'Luther is such a great man and he does so much for people. Okay, because he's your dad, I am not going to give you a ticket this time.' I said, 'No no,' but he insisted and said, 'No, no, it's okay.' He did not give me a ticket that day because I was Luther's daughter."

The longer you are in broadcasting, the more you get used to being in the public eye. Luther's wife, Mary, reflects that, even though Luther is well-known, to his family, he is still just Luther, Daddy, or Papaw.

From the personal collection of Luther and Mary Masingill

Luther with his two grandsons, Ian and Evan.

From the personal collection of Luther and Mary Masingill

Luther's grandsons Evan and Ian, May 2011.

"When you have a job like this and when you are working and constantly meeting people, you have to do your best and keep a smile on your face. But when Luther got home, it was a place where he could relax, a place where he did not have to answer the telephone or talk if he did not want to, a place where he could just be himself. He's a quiet man, and when he came home, he could relax and do all the things that other dads do, like help with the children or take care of little problems that arise around the house. When something would go wrong, he would always tell me he could fix it. I would ask him how he knew he could fix it, and his answer was always, 'Because I read *Popular Mechanics!*' [*laughs*]. But even the grandchildren got to experience a bit of Luther's notoriety when they were here in Chattanooga. They are older now, but when our grandson, Ian, was about five years old and the family was visiting from Texas, everywhere we went someone would greet

Luther or stop to talk to him. A short time later, we were out visiting them, and while out at some little hardware store, Ian looked up at his granddaddy and said, 'Papaw, nobody knows you out here, do they?' So Ian was pretty happy that day because he felt like he had his Papaw all to himself."

Luther misses part of his family that now lives in Texas, but he occasionally gets to have them all together.

Joanie and her family live out in Texas now, and Jeffrey is here in Chattanooga. It would be great to get to see Joanie and Mike and the boys more, but they don't get back too much. We had them here recently, but one of my grandsons had to work and wasn't able to make it due to his job. We missed him and wished he could have made it out to see his grandparents, but we understood. It was good to have them here. Joanie loves Texas, but she says, "Daddy, I think I love Chattanooga more."

Joanie never got tired of being with her dad and meeting people with him: "They would stop and want to speak to dad, and we would stay for a few moments and then drift away while Daddy was talking. We would go do whatever it was that we were out to do and Dad would catch up with us later. I always enjoyed meeting people who stopped to talk to Daddy, and like I said, I heard a million times: 'I remember the day you were born!' But I never got tired of it. I enjoyed it and I still do. Even now I hear it when I come home and am out with my dad. I am very proud of him and I miss seeing him. I wish we could see him more often. We came back to Chattanooga for a few years, but I have basically been away for 28 years. I wish he was able to spend more time with his grandsons, but as far as our relationship, it's great. We just don't get to see enough of each other."

BIG DOG, SMALL CAR.—Dr. Walter L. Martin, local veterinarian, today urged all citizens to have more consideration for their pets during vacation period. Dr. Martin said an increasing number of pets have suffered serious illnesses and even death from neglect by inconsiderate owners. To illustrate how not to take a vacation, Mr. and Mrs. Luther Masingill and their children, Joan and Jeffrey, pose with a Great Dane dog in a small sports car. Dr. Martin suggests that larger dogs be boarded in kennels rather than risk heatstroke, foreign objects flying up from the road and falling from an open car.—(Staff photo by Bill Truex.)

The Masingill family left to right: son Jeffrey, daughter Joan, Luther and Mary promoting pet safety, August 1969.

5
Luther the Chattanoogan

As a child listening to Luther on the radio, I often wondered where and how he lived. I wondered what his life was like when he wasn't on the air. I knew he lived in Chattanooga, but I wanted to know more about my childhood hero. As a young boy, we were out near Memorial Hospital, and my mom drove by Luther's neighborhood. I did not know exactly which house was his, but I knew he lived near Notre Dame High School in the Glenwood area of Chattanooga. I knew he had lived in the same house for many years. I've always been curious about his life, and even after I met him, questioned him incessantly about his life and childhood. One day I was doing a community service event at a school in the Avondale area and Luther drove me there. After I had spoken to the kids, I asked Luther about the school because I had remembered him talking about living in the East Chattanooga area. "This is where I went to elementary school," he said. I was happily surprised to speak at the school where so many years ago Luther had been a student too. We then hopped in his pickup truck and he drove me about two blocks over to Bradt Street. As we drove up to Luther's old house, I sat there in his truck thinking, "Man, if only these streets and this house could talk." I wish I could go back in time for even five minutes and see Luther playing in the backyard or see him playing with the boys in the neighborhood. What would that be like? A short time later, we went back to the house and I had the opportunity to sit there on the front porch

Photo by Holly Abernathy

Luther's childhood home at 1407 Bradt Street in East Chattanooga.

Photo by Holly Abernathy

Luther shares a few memories with James on the porch of his childhood
home in East Chattanooga.

Photo by Holly Abernathy

Luther and James in front of Luther's childhood home in East Chattanooga.

Photo by Holly Abernathy

Luther stepping off the porch of 1407 Bradt Street, his childhood home in East Chattanooga.

with him as he told me stories about growing up there. Sitting there with him on the porch was an amazing experience. As he told me a few stories of his childhood, he pointed to the church that he attended when he met his wife, Mary. I had heard some of these stories from Luther at the Sunny 92.3 WDEF-FM studios, but to actually be sitting there and talking to him where so many important events in his life took place was an amazing thing. There was so much of Luther's history all around us, and I could see in his eyes that it was bringing back some memories too.

I have many childhood memories of growing up in Chattanooga. I remember running behind the ice wagon and getting little slivers of ice. That was a lot of fun. We would cut grass around the neighborhood to try to make some money so we could go to town. We would use a sickle or a push mower, and you'd get 50 cents for doing yard work. You'd work your fanny off and would be sweating, and every once in a while, the people you were cutting the grass for would bring you out a cold glass of water. That was always nice and it helped. We lived in a good, warm community. People knew each other and helped each other. I enjoyed being brought up there in Avondale. I can remember in that house we had a little heater in the dining room and a monkey heater in the kitchen. A monkey heater is a little bitty cast iron heater that heats, and if you rig it up right, it will heat you some water. As a child, in the wintertime, you headed right for the kitchen or the dining room. You went wherever that heater was, but of course that's before we got our first electric water heater. I think it was a Hotpoint that we kept for at least 20 years, and it was still working when we moved out of the house. It was a good life.

As for growing up in Chattanooga, I lived on the streetcar line, right on the corner where the Boyce car ran. That was the car that ran out to East Chattanooga and back down to town. It cost us about a nickel. That was the streetcar that we took to downtown Chattanooga to go to the movies or to go shop at the five-and-dime downtown. In Avondale, trains used to come up and go through that tunnel where the Tennessee Valley Railroad Museum is now. The passenger trains went up that same route and through that same tunnel and off toward Knoxville. That was the freight train that went through your community. If you were poor, you would jump on the train as it was pulling out, and it would be running slow. Some of the boys in the neighborhood would climb up on it and start throwing off lumps of coal. In the wintertime, you used coal for heating your house, and in the summertime, you used it for cooking in your cook stove. It was funny seeing that coal come down off those trains. I said, "You throw it off; I'll pick it up." We did not sell it or anything. We just took it home. It was just a small amount and they did not even miss it.

Luther worked hard so he could make a little money to go downtown or to a theater in the area. He would watch movies, eat popcorn and candy bars, and stay there all afternoon and into the night. If he was downtown, he always had to remind himself to save enough money to ride the streetcar back home. The streetcar was the main mode of transportation back then. As a young boy, he would work all week for 50 or 75 cents just to go downtown on a Saturday and watch movies, sometimes three or four in a day.

You spent the entire Saturday going from one theater to another. You paid your dime, you got in and you saved enough for a Zagnut bar or maybe some popcorn. As a young boy, I used to go see the westerns and the serials. They charged ten cents and that's all you paid back then. Sometime later it became a quarter, but it was worth it. Over in East Chattanooga on Glass Street, there used to be a movie theater called the Rivoli Theater that we used to like to go to. We'd work all week to earn enough money to go to the Rivoli Theater. There aren't many businesses left in that area today, and of course the theater has been gone for years. I would go there often, and I remember one night in particular when I was coming home from the Rivoli Theater in East Chattanooga. I was just a young fellow, walking home by myself, and I began to hear a loud humming sound. There were no air conditioners in the windows at that time, and I did not know what I was hearing. As I turned around to look, suddenly I saw a beam of light behind me about a mile or two and in the air. There was a beam of light pointing down from the sky, a strong, bluish light. I was so puzzled and was wondering what in the world was shining down on me from the sky down here on Glass Street. It ended up being one of the Goodyear balloons or blimps, and he was making his way to the airport. He had turned his spotlight on, which looked like a big beam of light, because he was lost and was looking for the airport. He was heading in the right direction, but he was on the wrong side of the ridge. That sure did scare me that night as a young boy, seeing a big beam of light coming out of the sky around 10:30 at night when I should have already been home! That was a memorable evening coming home from the Rivoli Theater in East Chattanooga.

Chattanooga has changed tremendously over the years, even in my lifetime. You just did not go downtown much because there wasn't really a whole lot on offer, but now you've got the Tennessee Aquarium, the Creative Discovery Museum, restaurants, dinner theaters, movie theaters, the Riverwalk, and many other attractions downtown. These attractions were not available when I was a kid. Now, when I go downtown to see a movie, I think of Luther talking about how he used to smuggle Krystals in his pocket and take them to the movie theater downtown. When I was a kid, you only went to downtown Chattanooga when it was daylight. When it was dark, it was dangerous. I heard as a kid in elementary school, junior high and high school that you just did not want to find yourself at night in downtown Chattanooga. But Chattanooga has changed. The tourism industry is what transformed Chattanooga. Downtown is a drastically different place than it was in the past. You now have the shops downtown, the Riverfront, Frazier Avenue, the Walnut Street Pedestrian Bridge, Coolidge Park, and so much more. We did not have that here when I was a kid in Chattanooga. It was factory-based, industry-based, not a city built on tourism. Chattanooga was an industrial town, and while you can still see the shadow of Chattanooga's past, it is in stark contrast to what the city is today.

As a child, I knew of the big industrial plants around Chattanooga, such as Combustion Engineering, Standard-Coosa-Thatcher Co., Wheland Foundry, and Dixie Yarns. My dad worked at Standard-Coosa-Thatcher. You just knew that your friends' parents worked at these plants and that they supplied dinner, put food on the table for thousands of Chattanoogans. When I was around 15 years old, my dad called the family together to tell us he had lost his job. He told us, "Industry is going overseas. It's leaving Chattanooga; it's leaving the United States." It's funny the things you remember at these moments. My dad had told me once that when he hit his 25-year anniversary at the company he would get a gold watch. The day he told us he lost his job, I remember feeling disappointed that my dad was only two years away from getting his gold watch! It is obvious to me now that a gold watch was the last thing on my dad's mind at the time. His mind was on finding a job and feeding his family. My dad was out of work for about six months, and it was really rough on my family, but he finally got a job with National Posters and worked there until retirement. As a young man in high school, when all these plants moved or closed down or went bankrupt, I thought, "Man, I'm getting out of here when I graduate; there's nothing here to do."

Eventually tourism began to change the industrial landscape of Chattanooga. We already had Rock City and Ruby Falls, but the reputation of Chattanooga really started to turn around with the opening of the Tennessee Aquarium.

We, as residents, began to think that this might be a place where people could come with their families and enjoy some of the attractions and changes that were beginning to take root in our city. I look at Chattanooga today and I am proud of what it now has to offer. It's an exciting time and Chattanooga has come a long way. I am happy with what has taken place over the last couple decades and I know Luther is too. Few have seen firsthand how Chattanooga has evolved and how it continues to change and improve. Few people are alive today that know the history of Chattanooga like Luther.

Photo by Holly Abernathy

The Tennessee Aquarium.

Downtown was a different place back then. It was exciting because you had big five-and-dime stores with big candy counters and you had many choices, the way the candy was laid out. If you were so inclined, you could reach in and get a candy cherry or a marshmallow peanut right out of the display. I did that one time, and the young lady said, "Would you care to buy some candy?" I said, "No, ma'am. I'm just testing it, just trying it." She caught me. That was at Kress or McClellan's. They'll probably send me a bill for that now {laughs}.

We enjoyed the five-and-dime stores downtown, but further down at Ross' Landing on the riverfront, it was just nothing but cornfields. Farmers would grow corn along the riverbanks up to the roads that were close to the river. That's the way we lived. We lived out near one of those areas of cornfields that bordered the river and that bordered our property. It was just country; there was nothing there. Quaker Oats built a big plant over there and so did a lot of other companies over the years, but that was just flat land that was flooded before the dam was built. It was farmland, and corn was grown along the riverbanks.

As far as Chattanooga and industry, it was highly a manufacturing type of place here. There was Combustion Engineering and Wheland Company where my brother, James, worked that was out here on South Broad Street. Mary's daddy worked for Combustion Engineering Company. There was so much industry here and that made for a lot of pollution in the air. You did not want to breathe the air at times. A lot of this industrial pollution would settle on your car, and as the dew worked it's way in or a light rain would come, it would take all that pollution that had fallen on your car and cause it to rust. So you'd have a rusty car after a short time. Eventually we lost the industry and I'm sorry for that. I just hated when all the industry moved, not just out of Chattanooga but out of our country. It moved to other countries, particularly China, and that I regret. I'm sorry and I miss Combustion, Wheland and all the other companies that left and moved, whatever they manufactured, to another country.

I have passed Wheland Foundry every day since 1993 while going to work. At the time, the WDEF Radio studios were just across the street from Wheland. Luther would sometimes point out how you could see the smoke coming from the smokestacks at Wheland Foundry from his studio window. One day Luther kept talking about a vibration he kept hearing. He would say, "Hey, listen to that. Do you hear that?" He called a few people to come listen, and it was really kind of hard to hear what he was talking about. It was so faint, but Luther had been sitting in the same studio on South Broad Street for a long time. He knew his studio and he knew when there was a vibration in it. Luther picked up the phone and he called this man that he knew over at Wheland Foundry. The man came over to Luther's studio, and Luther said, "There it is. Do you hear it?" This guy said, "Yeah, I do. I hear it. That's odd." He finally figured out that it was a piece of machinery over at Wheland that was causing the vibration in Luther's studio on South Broad Street. I did not know it at the time, but that man from Wheland Foundry was my future father-in-law. Years later, my wife, Christy, and I were sitting around the dinner table with Christy's mom and dad, Mr. and Mrs. Thau. Christy's dad proceeded to tell the story about being in Luther's studio to fix the vibration that day. I thought that was such a coincidence.

One of my fondest memories of Wheland Foundry is when I proposed to Christy. After dating for about two years, Christy and I had stopped seeing each other for about three weeks. I missed her so much during that time that I just couldn't stand it. I was being selfish and felt like I did not want to be tied down at the time, but I learned my lesson when I was without her during that short period. I realized for those three weeks that we were apart that I just did not want to live my life without her. Having decided to propose to her, I bought a ring and then stopped by Wheland Foundry to ask Christy's dad for his blessing. I'll never forget how nervous I was as I pulled up in Wheland Foundry's parking lot and asked to speak with Bernie Thau. They rang for Bernie, and after about two or three minutes of waiting in the lobby, he came out. "Well, hey!" he said as he came out in his hard hat and big working boots. I sort of gulped and said, "Hey, Mr. Thau. Can I talk to you out in the parking lot?" He kindly answered, "Sure, James. What's going on?" I think I had him a little nervous, trying to figure out what was going on. "I want to marry your daughter," I said. He looked up and he had tears in his eyes. "Well, I thought you guys had broken up," he said. I told him that I had learned in the last three weeks that I just couldn't live without his daughter. "You have my blessing," he said, a little teary-eyed and a bit choked up. He shook my hand, and the next day I proposed to his daughter.

Growing up, I was always a big baseball fan and loved to go to the Chattanooga Lookouts games. My uncle, who is around Luther's age, was a member of the "Knothole Gang." The owner of the Lookouts, Joe Engel, came up with a program where, instead of looking through a knothole in the fence to watch a baseball game, kids could watch the Chattanooga Lookouts games for free if they got good grades in school. Kids who met the criteria could be exclusive members of Joe Engel's Knothole Gang. Luther remembers it well:

Joe Engel, owner of the Chattanooga Lookouts, had what was called the Knothole Gang. It was for kids going to school, and if they kept their grades and attendance up and attended Sunday school on Saturday or Sunday, they were given a card granting them free access to all the Chattanooga Lookouts games. They could attend all the home games, providing they met those requirements. It was a great program.

Frank Cothran, Selma, Ala. ...39-36—75

GIRLS' NIGHT SLATED AT STADIUM MAY 31

Joe Engel has designated the game of May 31 as the night that all girls between the ages 9 through 14 will be admitted to Engel Stadium free. The Lookouts will be host to the Nashville Vols on that night.

Luther Massengill is in charge of the arrangements for the girls' night and will be present at the pass gate through which the girls will be admitted. May 31st is also the night that the Knothole Gang members may start using their season tickets. Members of the armed forces will also be honored on this night.

Image courtesy of WDEF-TV Archives

The Knothole Gang is mentioned in an early newspaper clipping. Luther is also mentioned as being "in charge of the arrangements for the girls' night out" at Engel Stadium.

As much as I love baseball and enjoy watching the Lookouts play, I also associate one of the most embarrassing moments of my life with a Lookouts game at Engel Stadium. It was an evening in 1996 with a record crowd, close to 11,000 people. Engel Stadium was packed, and I had the opportunity to throw out the first pitch with Frank Gifford, NFL Hall of Fame player and sports broadcaster. I had played baseball for eight years so I knew how to pitch a ball. I wasn't a pitcher, but I loved baseball, and so it was no big deal to pitch or to throw a straight-line baseball and to throw it fast. They announced my name as I got up there on the mound: "James Howard from Sunny 92.3!" Everyone was cheering me on. The crowd was hyped up, screaming and cheering because Kathy Lee Gifford had just finished singing the national anthem. I was on the mound, and the Lookouts catcher was putting his fist in his catcher's mitt, looking at me and pointing at me to "hit it right there." So I reared back and I threw that ball; only, it bounced about two feet in front of me and rolled on the ground to the catcher's mitt. The people in the record crowd started booing, all 11,000 of them. I have never, ever felt so humiliated in my entire life. After I threw the ball, if that's what you want to call it, they announced Frank Gifford and the crowd went crazy. He came out there and just drilled his ball to the catcher. As I was jogging off the field with Frank Gifford, he tossed me his ball and said, "Don't worry about it, Kid; we all goof up sometimes." When I went to sit in the stands with my dad, a couple of guys started taunting me, saying, "I hope you fly better than you pitch!" They obviously had seen the media coverage just two weeks prior that I had set a national speed record after touching down at every airport in the state of Tennessee. The evening was humiliating. I ended up leaving because I felt so bad. On my way home, a guy in front of me ran out of gas on I-75. As I was helping him get his car off the road, I told him the story of what had just taken place at Engel Stadium. "Man, just the opportunity to have thrown out the first pitch, whether you bomb it or not, wow, what an honor, especially with Frank Gifford!" he reassured me. "Thank you for telling me that," I said gratefully. "Here, here's the baseball. I don't want any remembrance of this game. You made me feel better. Here's the game ball." Later, I told Luther about it and he said sympathetically, "Yeah, I heard." He pretty much told me what the guy on I-75 told me: "Appreciate the opportunity. It's just baseball. If you bomb the first pitch, people are going to boo you. They're going to boo the President if he does that." Luther made me feel better about the whole situation and helped me to take it less seriously.

To this day, I enjoy going to the Chattanooga Lookouts games and had the pleasure of taking Luther's grandsons to a game once. Luther used to be the public address announcer at the Lookouts games, and while a fan, he did not often play the game of baseball.

I did not play too much. I couldn't hit it very well. Being in radio, I was also a bit afraid of the ball hitting me in the mouth. Many times I was asked to play on a team for a charity benefit, and I would, but only after asking them where they were going to put me. "Well, the place that gets the least action is out in center field," they'd say. So I told them, "Alright, give me the catcher's equipment – you know, the cup, the mitt, the gloves and the mask – and I'll play center field for you. That's the only way {laughs}."

I really enjoyed being out at Engel Stadium. It was really something. If you remember far enough back like I do, you remember Jim Lemon; you remember a lot of the players who played in Engel Stadium at exhibition games or played for the Lookouts as they were either going up or coming down the ladder of fame in baseball. It was a great time in the history of the Chattanooga Lookouts.

It would be impossible to discuss the history of Chattanooga without highlighting the name John T. "Jack" Lupton of the Lupton family, longtime residents of Lookout Mountain, Tennessee. If you're here long enough, you'll eventually hear the story of how Jack's grandfather, along with a couple of partners, started a bottling business that was eventually handed down to Jack's father. The partners paid $1.00 for the right to bottle Coca-Cola. Over time, the operation grew into one

Luther on the front of the Chattanooga Baseball Club Official Score Book.
"WDEF: The Station of Public Service."

of the largest in the world, mostly due to Coca-Cola sales. Jack's father died and Jack assumed control of the business. In 1986, after a lack of interest from his children in taking over and having served many years on the board of directors of the Coca-Cola Co. in Atlanta, Jack sold the business to Coca-Cola for a reported $1.4 billion. Jack then began focusing on what has been called the "revitalization" of Chattanooga. He is most notably credited with playing a crucial role in the development of the Tennessee Aquarium.

Jack died peacefully on Sunday, May 16, 2010, at the age of 83. Jack had a great love for his community, and it was evident in his work and philanthropic efforts in the city. According to his obituary in the *Chattanooga Times Free Press*, "Even greater than his love for Coke was Jack's love for his home community. The three things he was most proud of were his involvement with the Lyndhurst Foundation, the Tennessee Aquarium and the Honors Golf Course, all of which helped change the face of a decaying city and none of which would have happened without him."

Over the years, I've had people tell me that Luther was a good friend of Jack Lupton. I remember Luther would joke about Jack Lupton sending him a blank check, but some people really thought that he was being serious. It wasn't until recently that Luther admitted that Jack never really did and that he was only joking.

On my 80th birthday, I said on the air that Jack had sent me a blank check with his signature on it and that he said, "You fill it out for whatever you want and 'Happy Birthday, Luther!'" That was a bunch of bull. He did not do that. He ran into me a few days afterwards and said, "What do you mean getting on the air, saying I sent you a blank check? Do you need some money?" "Well, no, Jack," I said. "I don't need any money." He laughed and said, "Well, don't do it again," and walked off.

Jack and I knew each other as teenagers. We would go swimming together at the YMCA, which was located on Georgia Avenue, just a couple of doors down from the Volunteer Building. We would swim and exercise together. We would also sun bathe on top of the Volunteer Building and sometimes get so blistered up there. We worked in the same building, the Volunteer Building down on Georgia

Avenue. The radio studios were on the 4th floor, and he worked for his father in his father's office during this time, which I believe was on the 7th floor. Of course I've mentioned how my good friend, Buddy Houts, was always joking and making us laugh. Well, working in the same building, we would run into Jack and his father every once in a while on the elevator. One day, we were getting on, going down, and Jack and his daddy were already on the elevator. Buddy and I got on and Buddy said, "You know, Luther, they didn't know if anybody had been killed in the room until they saw the blood coming out from under the door." And I said, "Really?" About that time the 2nd floor door opened, and Jack and his daddy got off the elevator. Later, they told me they were just looking at each other after they got off the elevator, wondering what in the world he was talking about — who had just been killed in the Volunteer Building? Of course we told him later that we were only joking.

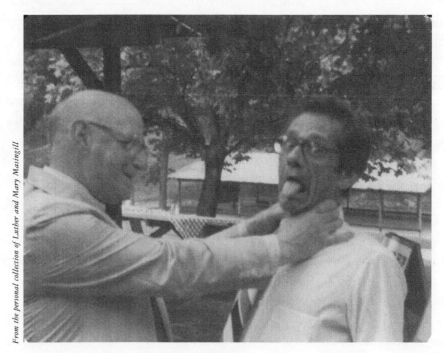

Luther and Buddy Houts, May 1980.

*Over the years, Jack and I would run into each other, and he'd mention some-
thing about listening to me on the radio. "Hey, I listened to you and I like your
music," he'd say. I used to ask him who his favorite artists were, and at the time,
he'd mention people like Perry Como and Bing Crosby. He also liked Dinah Shore.
He liked all the old-timers. He stopped me once when he was downtown on his
way to Yacoubian to buy some clothing as I was just coming from K-Mart where I
bought my suit {laughs}. He stopped me at an intersection after apparently hearing
something I'd said on the radio about him. He was funny as he pulled up and said,
"What did you say about me on the air?" I said, "Jack, it was good. I love you for
what you did for this city with the aquarium. I love what it is doing and what it
will do for this city. I just appreciate it so much and I love you for it — and I like
your suits too. When you get another suit and you're tired of that one, I'd like to have
it" {laughs}. He just laughed and pulled off. Seeing the aquarium come together
and what it has done for this town was a big thrill. I gave Jack Lupton credit for it
on the air quite a few times, and even though he's passed on, I am still appreciative of
him and what he's done for our city, especially in regards to the Tennessee Aquarium.*

My first experience with the Tennessee Aquarium was when it opened
in 1992. I was a senior in high school and there was a buzz of excitement
because the aquarium was due to open soon. Our senior class needed to take
some pictures, so we did it at the Tennessee Aquarium. A little archway
bridge was built right out front, and we were paired up with a "sweetheart"
for photos. That seems like it was yesterday.

The Tennessee Aquarium has done a lot for Chattanooga. I believe it's
what put Chattanooga on the map. We now have something to offer, and
I think the aquarium was the first big thing we introduced that helped
define Chattanooga as a global city. I love meeting families who are visiting
not only from the Southeast, but from all over the country. They are generally so impressed with our city. I've met people from Birmingham who tell
me they really did not know much about Chattanooga, but they enjoyed
being here so much. "This is our first visit and we love it," they'll say. I've
spoken with people from Detroit who were in the car business but moved
here due to the Volkswagon plant that's now in town. "We've heard about

the Chattanooga Choo Choo," they'll say, "but we did not know about the Tennessee Aquarium. It's a wonderful place to visit."

As a boy, I loved going to the Chattanooga Choo Choo. Hollywood has glamorized train stations, and you cannot help but get nostalgic when taking a stroll around the Choo Choo. Not much has changed. Sometimes I'll take my girls over for a walk around the grounds, and you can still hear the big band music playing out over the speakers. Occasionally you'll hear the "Chattanooga Choo Choo" by Glenn Miller and His Orchestra, the memorable tune that made our city and the historic landmark famous. The lobby looks much the same as it did years ago, and you can easily get a sense of the historic value of the Chattanooga Choo Choo. Terminal Station on Market Street has been called Chattanooga's "Gateway" and has greeted Presidents Theodore Roosevelt, Woodrow Wilson, and Franklin D. Roosevelt. I can only imagine what it was like back then. As a kid, I remember seeing a plaque with a black and white picture on it of the last train exiting the Chattanooga Choo Choo as an official train depot in 1970. Fortunately, investors intervened and this historic Chattanooga landmark was preserved. Today it's used as a hotel and conference center.

The Chattanooga Choo Choo is one of the great places to see in Chattanooga. Many years ago, it was just an exciting place to be. There were people moving here and there and just hustling about. I'll always remember boarding the train there at the station with Mary and riding to New York. We really enjoyed riding the train to New York and to Washington when we had the opportunity. In later years, they refurbished the establishment and made hotel rooms out of the cars. One car would consist of, I believe, two rooms. We never did rent a room in a car, but you could do that and it has become pretty popular. You could actually live in the car, bathe in the car, go to the bathroom in the car and sleep in the car. You could go to the Choo Choo and just have a good time. And we've been there for banquets and have had some of our high school reunions there. It's always interesting to talk to some of the people you went to school with and discuss the changes and improvements that the Chattanooga Choo Choo has made over the years.

The Walnut Street Bridge is another one of Chattanooga's most popular attractions. It's one of the world's longest pedestrian bridges and a favorite of residents and visitors alike. The Walnut Street Bridge was constructed between 1889 and 1891 and spans 2,370 feet, but it was closed to all traffic in 1978. According to the *Historic American Engineering Record*, it was constructed "to replace cumbersome ferries." The bridge opened for pedestrian use only in the early 1990s and was listed on the National Register of Historic Places in 1990. I am so thankful for the efforts that were taken to turn it into the leisurely and scenic attraction it is today. The views afforded from the bridge out over the Tennessee River are truly breathtaking. I love walking the Walnut Street Bridge with my family as often as I can, knowing it is a defining icon in Chattanooga's landscape. Luther has enjoyed walking the bridge with Mary as well. Some mornings when he comes into work and I ask, "What did you do last evening?", he will tell me how he and Mary walked the Walnut Street Bridge and spent time enjoying the riverfront.

Before the Walnut Street Bridge became a pedestrian bridge, we drove over it in our automobiles. I remember driving over that bridge many times before it became the walking bridge that it is today. For a long time, they closed it to traffic due to structural issues. No one would ever even look at it, and I remember people asking what they were going to do with "that old bridge." When they finally finished redoing it and making it what it is today, it was a jewel. People walked on it and just marveled at what they had done. There are plaques that run all along the bridge with the names of some of the supporters of the bridge. I put our name in brass down on one of the plaques, but then it disappeared during the time they were being stolen. I'm not sure if it has ever been put back up. But the Walnut Street Bridge is a wonderful place to enjoy the views of Chattanooga. That was a really nice event when they completed it, and it's a very nice addition to our city.

Photo by Holly Abernathy

The Walnut Street Bridge.

Photo by Holly Abernathy

Coolidge Park.

Coolidge Park in downtown Chattanooga was named in honor of World War II Medal of Honor recipient Charles H. Coolidge. The park is on the north shore of the Tennessee River and sits below a portion of the Walnut Street Pedestrian Bridge. As a kid, I remember this area being nothing but woods. Today, it is one of the most popular parks in all of Chattanooga and has an interactive water feature where children are often seen playing, as well as curving walkways and the beautifully restored, hand-carved Coolidge Park Carousel. The change is remarkable. When I went to my junior prom in 1991, we were in that area for dinner, and where Coolidge is today was overgrown with trees and weeds. There was a restaurant and some apartment buildings, but at the foot of the Walnut and Market Street Bridges there was nothing but a wooded area. The grounds have changed tremendously and it is hard to imagine Coolidge Park being anything other than what it is today.

Down in what is Coolidge Park now, there was a Marine Corp building occupied by the marines where they did their drills. They had their meetings there, and there were one or two other places, but that's the one I remember the most. They moved out when the carousel was put in the park. They just made something so beautiful out of it. They've had the concerts there, they've had all kinds of events there in Coolidge Park, and it was of course named after a very fine, great soldier who served our country, Mr. Coolidge. He's soft-spoken and just as kind and sweet a guy as you'd ever want to meet. He owns a printing company here in town, Chattanooga Printing and Engraving. It is a wonderful park named after Mr. Coolidge, and they have turned it into something beautiful. It's one more thing our city can be proud of.

So many things have changed over the years in Chattanooga. The years have gone by fast, but this city has added a lot. In other parts of town, there are still some empty buildings and some room for growth, but a lot has changed and a lot has been added. There is also a lot that is missing — things that are now gone, things that will never come back. I think we have become a tourist city, and there are companies that are here that wouldn't be here had it not been for the Tennessee Aquarium and many of the other attractions. So here we are now; we've got this fine, wonderful place. It's a great place to live. People have asked me over the years, "Why don't you go somewhere else?" I've had offers, yes, but Chattanooga is home and I love this place. I really do.

6

Luther the Coworker and Friend

I have worked with Luther for more than 20 years. I've gone from hearing him on the radio as a child to working alongside him every day. Not only do I have the distinct pleasure of working with Luther, a legendary broadcaster and my childhood hero, I have the honor of calling him my friend. Over the years, that friendship has developed in both times of seriousness and in times of laughter. One of our more light-hearted interactions was the infamous "spider incident." A spider was on the ceiling in the studio. Taking a dislike to spiders, I killed it. I examined the dead spider, did some research, and determined it was a brown recluse. I notified the rest of the morning show crew of my discovery.

Luther soon returned to his studio and started his community announcements live on the radio. I went into his studio and began to tickle the back of his head and neck with a yardstick. I have never seen him move so fast. His arms were flailing and he came up out of his chair, grabbed me with both hands by the shirt collar and thrust me into a corner. I had never seen him that angry! He was so startled by the incident that he said he almost "knocked his own brains out." The "spider incident" is one of many times we have joked around with one another. Of course we have disagreed during moments in our careers, but that is the business side. Modern radio has its conflicts, but that is expected. Throughout my life with Luther, I have learned so much from him. He will always be my mentor and my friend. During an interview, Luther described his recollection of our first meeting:

My first encounter with James, the practical joker of all practical jokers, who often laughs at his own misfortune, was when he was a cameraman. He was doing some camera work for WDEF Television and we were in the same building. The radio station was upstairs and he would come up and watch us as we were broadcasting. I kind of felt like he had a little more interest in radio than he did in television, but he was doing both and we were glad to see that. He was an eager beaver and would hang around the studios quite a bit. He would come in and ask, "Can I sit and watch you a while?" And I'd say, "Yes, what's your name?" "James Howard," he'd reply. I remember that. So that's the way he worked his way in. He showed a great interest in the work and so he was later hired. I was glad because he was a good worker.

As the years have gone by, James has been a great guy to work with and to have around. He's a good guy — he really is — and he's a good worker. Anything you ask him to do, he'll do. He is not one of these who starts giving you excuses. He is not one of those fellows. We used to have them in radio where they'd complain about something and the next day they're not on duty. He can sometimes get a little aggravating with all his practical jokes. Just a few minutes ago, as a matter of fact, I was getting ready to throw away some cake that was leftover in the studio from yesterday. He watched me drop it into the garbage can and then said, "Luther, I wanted one more bite of that." Just for that I made him take it out of the garbage and eat it! But James is a good guy and I consider him a good friend.

One of the recurring characteristics I hear people mention when they describe Luther is generosity. I can personally attest to Luther's generosity in so many ways over the years. He gives without expecting anything in return. I have known Luther for over 20 years and we have worked side by side together for 13. I have learned that when you mention something, even before you are finished talking, Luther is already thinking about a way to help you. I once mentioned that I had a leaking toilet, and before I was home that afternoon, Luther called me to let me know someone was coming over in 15 minutes to fix the toilet. "I got this guy that's going to fix your toilet. He is going to be over there in 15 minutes. Are you going to be there?" he asked. His thoughtfulness

Photo by Holly Abernathy

The Sunny 92.3 WDEF-FM morning team: Gene, Kim, James and Luther.

Photo by Holly Abernathy

James and Luther at Luther's 85th birthday party, March 2007.

Photo by Holly Abernathy

James and Luther joking around backstage prior to speaking to the UTC student body, March 2012.

Photo by Holly Abernathy

Luther, Mary and James looking over some of the photos from Luther and Mary's wedding day, January 2012.

Photo by Holly Abernathy

James and Luther after Luther's 90th birthday party, March 2012.

is what I have experienced during my whole radio career with him. From what I've observed, it is a win-win situation where he wants the repairman to get a little extra money. He wants the business for him. At the same time, he wants the person with the problem to have a resolution. He is a good friend that derives joy from helping people. I have experienced his generosity in my own life and I have observed it at work in the lives of many others as well. Not only is he generous with his resources, he is generous with his time and has a genuine concern for the well being of others.

I have experienced Luther's concern the many times I have gone to visit our local troops in war zones in the Middle East. Some of the best memories I have with Luther are getting back from my trips and sharing with him my stories of being in that part of the world. I have gone for many years now to visit our local troops during the holidays, to bring a piece of home to them while they are serving our country over in the Middle East. I love to sit down with Luther and tell him about my experiences in Iraq and Afghanistan. When I started talking about taking that first trip to Iraq, he became deeply concerned, not only for my safety, but for the safety of my family. I know he loves me, but he also loves Christy and the girls and checks on them when I am gone. And every time I've gone to Iraq and Afghanistan, he's been there to see me off.

I recall the day James told all of us goodbye at the airport when he was going on one of his trips to visit our troops in Afghanistan. A lot of his friends were there and there were some listeners and viewers. It was very sentimental. His mom and dad were there along with his immediate family. It was good to be there with him and with Lucy, Gracie and Christy. It was just good being with them and watching as we waved goodbye, not knowing if he was going to return. That was a bad place over there — still is — but he did get back and will probably go again. If he does, we will miss him and hope, once again, for his safe return.

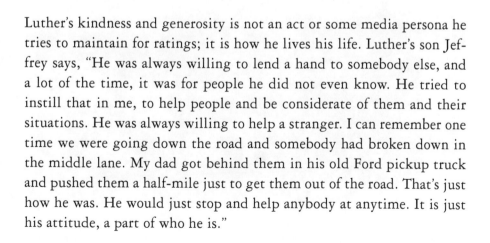

Luther's kindness and generosity is not an act or some media persona he tries to maintain for ratings; it is how he lives his life. Luther's son Jeffrey says, "He was always willing to lend a hand to somebody else, and a lot of the time, it was for people he did not even know. He tried to instill that in me, to help people and be considerate of them and their situations. He was always willing to help a stranger. I can remember one time we were going down the road and somebody had broken down in the middle lane. My dad got behind them in his old Ford pickup truck and pushed them a half-mile just to get them out of the road. That's just how he was. He would just stop and help anybody at anytime. It is just his attitude, a part of who he is."

Photo by Holly Abernathy

Luther and James at the Chattanooga Airport before James left for the Middle East to be embedded with the troops, December 2009.

Photo courtesy of James Howard

James, U.S. Senator Bob Corker and Luther at the Chattanooga Airport prior to James' Afghanistan trip, December 2010.

Jeffrey also mentioned the value Luther places on humor and how so many do not know this about him. "Another thing a lot of people may not realize about my dad is his sense of humor. He is real quick and witty, and he doesn't bring that out a lot, especially when he is on the radio. He is all business when he is on the radio, but when you get around him, he has a really great sense of humor."

Luther is indeed one of the funniest men I know. Humor and friendship are very important to him and the two intermingle in Luther's personal life.

Just about all my life I've been attracted to people with humor. I guess the one person that stands out more for that than anybody else was my friend, Buddy Houts. He was such a funny fellow, always cutting up and pulling practical jokes. I found him so amusing and he kept me laughing all the time. So it was a pleasure to work with him. Everything he said, just the way he looked at you, you would get so tickled. There would be times when we'd be driving along on the Market Street Bridge. He'd be driving and he'd slow down right in the middle of the bridge and stick his arm out like he's going to make a turn right in the middle of the bridge. He knew that tickled me. He's also the one that rode a motorcycle down the hallway of the old Central High School when it was located on Dodds Avenue. He did so many things and brought so many laughs to the individuals in the classroom. He was just a funny guy, and he was the same way when he started working for WDEF. Later on, he left us and went with the newspaper to write a column about cars. He was an expert on cars, old and new. He would go to these automobile meetings in Detroit, and the president of the company was always there at the meeting, along with their chief engineers, and Henry Ford would call on him. Mr. Ford would call on Buddy and there were times when he never did call on anybody else. He would be standing and talking to Buddy, telling him what they hoped to perform in the upcoming year. He'd say, "Buddy, Buddy Houts, back there in the back, stand up. You're kind of short, aren't you?" He knew Buddy was funny and Buddy laughed at his jokes. Buddy wasn't that short, but that was just a joke from Mr. Ford. But Mr. Ford would say, "Buddy, haven't you got a question for me?" and Buddy would ask him a question, something that was highly technical and Mr. Ford would answer it. It just tickled him that he was one of the only writers to be questioned in that session in a meeting in Detroit. Buddy was a fan of the Ford.

Another time I remember with Buddy was when this elderly lady brought us a cake down to the station. Sometimes listeners would bring things to us. They don't do it as much as they used to and we don't encourage it here at our station, although some stations do. So sometimes a listener would bake a cake and bring it down to the station for us. They would work all afternoon on it and bring it down to you the next morning. A lady did this for us once and she happened to be a tuberculosis patient at one of the hospitals. She got out, but she had access to a kitchen in the hospital where she'd made this cake for me and Buddy and the morning show staff. So she brought it in, put it down and left. Afterwards we thanked her on the air. As the staff came in, there was one person in particular who saw it on Buddy's desk in his work area in the control room. He said, "Yeah! Cake! All right!" Buddy knew he loved goodies – especially cake – that folks would bring down to the station. "Yeah, hey, have a piece. A lady brought it in. She made it herself. She worked all afternoon on it," Buddy said. So the staff member took a bite of it and said, "Oh, this is good. This is good!" Buddy said, "Yeah, that's good. I'm glad you like it because she's such a sweet lady and she brought it to the staff. It's unusual, though, that she baked that. They've asked her many times, but she won't wear a mask when she bakes and mixes the stuff together for a cake. She coughs a lot – a lot. It's the worst coughing I've ever heard and it happens when she's preparing the cake and she still won't put on a mask!" Buddy told him that while he was standing there eating a bite. I remember that guy just walked over to the wastebasket and very quietly dropped whatever he had in his mouth in the trash. Only later would Buddy tell them he was only joking.

Mary Masingill remembers Buddy with great fondness as well. "Buddy was a great friend," she tenderly reflects. "We used to love to meet up with him and his wife because he was just a bundle of fun. Buddy was a good friend. He kept our lives happy."

From the personal collection of Luther and Mary Masingill

Luther and his dear friend Buddy Houts.

My Life With Luther

you find for me a single passage of Scripture which *forbids* polygamy?"

"Certainly," replied Twain. " 'No man can serve two masters.' "

—Louis Untermeyer, *A Treasury of Laughter* (Simon and Schuster)

LUTHER MASINGILL, of WDEF radio in Chattanooga, called his friend Buddy Houts, a newspaper editor, and asked if he'd been hang-gliding lately. Buddy answered, "Not since I heard about the two farmers hunting in the Smokies."

"What do you mean?" asked Luther.

Buddy said, "The farmers aimed and fired. One said, 'What in the

world kind of bird was that?' The other replied, 'I don't know, but I sure made him drop that man he was carrying.' " —WDEF, Chattanooga

. . . AND THEN there was the Mother Superior who ruled out perfumes. She was a no-nun-scent type. —Shelby Friedman

PAT MURPHY worked at the local brewery. One day while stirring a vat of beer he lost his balance and fell in. Pat's wife was called to the brewery and was given the awful news of his drowning. After regaining her composure she allowed that she assumed his death was at least merciful and quick.

The foreman shook his head, saying, "I don't know about that, Mrs. Murphy. He got out twice to go to the bathroom." —Ed Somers, quoted by Gene Brown in Danbury, Conn., *News-Times*

AN ATTORNEY who journeyed to California to try an important case promised to wire his partner the moment a decision was announced. At long last the wire came and it read: "Justice has triumphed." His partner in New York wired back: "Appeal at once."

—Mary H. Waldrip in Dawson County, Ga., *Advertiser and News*

A TOURIST visiting a castle in Scotland told the laird that he had just seen the family ghost in an upstairs corridor. "Did it give you a start?" the lord of the castle asked.

"To tell you the truth," said the tourist, "I didn't need one."

—Quoted in *Management Digest*

I HAVE one of those doctors who don't take anything seriously. One time I went to see him with chills and a fever. I said, "What would you call this?" He looked over his glasses and asked me, "Do you want the technical name?" I replied, "Of course I want the technical name." He said, "Shake 'N Bake." —*Orben's Current Comedy*

AN ARAB SHEIK returned home from a vacation in the United States. A fellow sheik asked him, "What impressed you most about the Americans?"

"Their salesmen," he replied, strapping on his skis. —Joey Russell in *Modern People*

Have you a joke for "Laughter, the Best Medicine"? See page 3.

120

Luther and Buddy's constant joking made it into *The Readers Digest*, November 1979.

Luther and Buddy Houts hard at work.

Luther and Buddy Houts during a station promotion.

Buddy Houts.

Luther has not only been a good friend to me; he has the reputation of being a good friend to others. Luther's daughter Joanie recalls watching her dad do things for others on many occasions. "My dad is somebody who is committed. When he has a strong belief or a strong commitment to something, he is committed to it and he doesn't let something stand in the way. You know, he always had his little things about 'returning good for evil' and 'do unto others'. He just lived his life by the Golden Rule and it has worked. I just go back and I think about things like Ms. Harrell, his teacher in elementary school, just things like that. A lot of people would not take the time to do the things he did for her, and things that he does for other people that they, many times, never even know about. And he doesn't want any recognition. He just does things because it is the right thing to do."

Ms. Harrell was Mary's teacher in Elementary School as well. Luther's wife, Mary, describes Ms. Harrell as "a really precious lady". Mary recalls a time when Luther extended special care to Ms. Harrell: "Luther and I both went to Avondale Grammar School as kids. My teacher in the second grade there was named Ms. Harrell. She lived in a house in Avondale on Wilson Street. She was born in a four- or five-bedroom house and it was heated with a fireplace and a coal-burning stove. She lived there in that house until she passed away. She was almost 100 years old. Luther would go over and make sure that she had food and groceries. In the wintertime, he would take her coal so that she could keep her house warm. She was there so long that it almost got to be a problem trying to find coal companies that sold lump coal that you could put in a stove and burn for heat. Luther finally talked her into getting a kerosene heater, but she would still get coal when she could and build a fire in her coal heater. She lived the rest of her life that way, but Luther always made sure she was taken care of and had what she needed. When you are in grammar school and your teacher is your authority, you don't think about, years later, being the one taking care of her. So it was just a sweet thing he did, making sure that she was okay every day."

Since I've known him, Luther has been a kind, generous, and caring friend. He has been the same friend to me and to my family for many years, and I've watched him treat others with the same kindness and respect. When you hear someone talking about Luther, the recurring themes are always humor, kindness and generosity. While I wish I could have included them all, here are a few words that some of Luther's friends and coworkers wanted to share with him and about him.

David Carroll and Luther, March 2012.

David Carroll
News Anchor, WRCB-TV Channel 3, Chattanooga, TN
David worked with Luther while at WDEF-TV from 1983 to 1987. He has filled in for him frequently on WDEF-FM since 1987.

I used to call Luther for career advice when I was a teenager. He was always very polite and helpful. When I was a child growing up in a family grocery store in Bryant, Alabama, customers would come in to stock up on bread and milk because "Luther" said it was going to snow. I thought this Luther guy must be pretty powerful!

Luther, I would like to say thanks for just being yourself and for understanding that the key to a successful career in communications is helping people, every day, as often as possible. You told me a few years ago that your "secret" was trying to help someone between every song that you played. You certainly succeeded, and that's why you're the all-time "King of Morning Radio"!

Photo by Holly Abernathy

Gene Lovin and Luther, March 2012.

Gene Lovin
Morning Show Producer for James, Kim (Lyons Carson) and Luther (The Sunny 92.3 WDEF Morning Show Team), WDEF-FM

Gene has worked with Luther in various capacities over the years, most recently as producer of the Sunny 92.3 Morning Show.

I have been in radio for more than 35 years and in the Chattanooga market for a long time, up and down the dial. When I first came to Chattanooga, I worked at another radio station, and the idea was that every station wanted to beat Luther. Every morning man that ever came into market at any of the radio stations, their goal was to beat Luther. I don't know that it has ever happened but that was pretty much it. That was the intent. There were actually people brought in out of larger markets into Chattanooga to take on Luther. He had his appeal and radio programmers always thought that they could crack that appeal and they never did. It never happened. To this day, even when I go out and people find out that I work with WDEF, it is always "that's Luther's station."

When I got into radio, the formats were very tight and very restricted. The stations were very formatted, whereas Luther was more personable and more personality-oriented. He was more involved in the community and had more of an outreach to the listeners.

Luther is a very giving and sincere person, but he is Luther. If he knows of somebody in need, he really tries to do something to help without wanting any recognition. I worked with a couple guys at a station in Atlanta when Luther went down there to do a Mayfield commercial. Luther overheard one of the morning team guys talking about his process of adopting two or three children. When production was complete with the Mayfield commercial, he walked over and slid the guy a few hundred dollars and said, "Here, this will help you get those kids." They were shocked. They had heard of Luther before, but they had just met him that day. I am sure there are a lot of stories that even his coworkers don't know about. He has done things for me, too, over the years and I've tried to refuse, but then you realize his gifts are given out of love and his feelings are hurt if you don't accept his generosity.

Many times people will ask me what Luther is like off the air. They have this perception of what he is like on the radio, but there is so much more to Luther. He is a genuine person, and he has many layers. He is serious and sincere, yet a funny and generous person that really does care about others. Many people might think his traits are "old school" because of the way he openly shows his care and love for others, but Luther is genuine. I am fortunate to work with him.

Robin Daniels
Music Director, WDEF-FM

Robin has worked with Luther while filling in as newscaster on WDEF-FM.

There are many things Chattanoogans may not know about Luther. He's picky about studio maintenance, such as making sure all the light bulbs are working and that all air filters are changed on a timely basis. More importantly, many may not know about his generosity.

One Saturday morning, a co-worker was late for work because he had two flat tires. He changed the first one, drove another couple of miles, and suffered a second. The guy ended up running about 20 blocks to get to the station. Most of the air staff, including Luther, was on hand at an event at the Chattanooga Trade and Convention Center that morning. I was getting ready to return to the station to get another piece of equipment when Luther called me aside, pressed a $100 bill in my palm, and told me to quietly give it to our ill-fated co-worker. This was a generous act from a most generous man.

Patti Sanders
Assistant Program Director and Mid-day Hostess, WDEF-FM

Patti's mid-day radio show has followed the Luther morning show on WDEF-FM since 1997.

My first experience with Luther was when I was hired at Sunny 92.3 WDEF Radio and was being introduced to my new team members. As I prepared to meet Luther for the very first time, he was spackling a small hole in the bathroom at the radio station!

Over the years, I've learned Luther is a man who loves Moon Pies and Little Debbie snack cakes, the roll-up kind with raspberry inside, with which I love to surprise him. More importantly, he helps out in our community in ways we cannot even imagine. I was in a local post office one day, and the postal employee at the counter told me Luther had been a customer at the post office the previous day. He said Luther had gotten his weed-whacker out of the back of his truck and week-whacked a little bit of grass in front of the post office because he thought "it needed it"! I'm certain he was just trying to save someone else the trouble.

Luther, I admire you greatly for your many decades with the same employer, always at work, always on time, and rarely taking days off. You have a work ethic that is so very rare and almost unheard of and one I try to emulate. You are classy, gracious, kind and funny. I take care of you and you take care of me and I cannot wait for my morning hug from you tomorrow. I love you dearly.

Photo courtesy of Patti Sanders

James, Luther and Patti.

Doris Ellis
Program and Community Affairs Director, WDEF News 12
Doris has worked with Luther at WDEF-TV since 1967.

Luther has a heart as big as his radio and TV audience. There are so many stories I could share, having known Luther all these years, but one thing that is constant is his generosity. It never fails. If we were collecting for someone in need or for a specific charity, Luther would always slip us a little money in private to help out. That is just Luther. For years, I have kept a candy drawer in my office just for him. It's a regular ritual for Luther to stop by every morning and prowl in the drawer for his favorite, Butterfinger or Mint Chocolate Milky Way. Then, he's on his way to share his candy with some of the others down the hall.

Interestingly, he has always been "Mister Fix-It." If the station had a leaking faucet or a commode running in the bathroom, he would either fix it or get someone to fix it. If a light bulb needed changing, he would change it. Another time, I looked out the window of the lobby and saw a load of cut wood in the back of Luther's truck. I asked him if he thought it was going to be a cold winter. He just laughed and said he was delivering it to some of the elderly women in his church. He jokingly said he had been doing it for so many years that he was now a lot older than the elderly women he was delivering the wood to. Luther has always had a great sense of humor. It was very hard to pull something over on Luther, but Neil Miller, who worked at the station for many years, always tried. Neil truly was a genuine prankster. There was a parking garage across the street from the Volunteer Life Building (the first location of the WDEF studios, 1954-1956). Luther's radio booth was located on one of the upper floors with a window facing the parking garage. Neil and one of his associates staged a very loud argument on the street below and then proceeded to the upper deck of the garage where they had a dummy stashed. The two continued their loud argument and a staged fight ensued. One fell down out of the sight of Luther, and the next thing that was seen was the dummy falling from the garage deck. You can just imagine Luther's anxiety when he thought he had just witnessed a murder being committed right there on top of the parking garage. Neil got a big belly laugh at getting one over on Luther and remembering the day he almost scared Luther to death!

We have always kidded Luther that we have recorded all his shows and have categorized them into types of weather days, so that long after he's gone, we will still be playing the Luther show and no one would ever suspect he's no longer around. It adds new meaning to "infinity and beyond."

Photo courtesy of WDEF-TV Archives

Doris Ellis and Luther.

Holly Abernathy
Freelance Writer and Photographer, Nashville, TN

Holly worked with Luther during her employment at WDEF-FM as promotions director and overnight DJ in the late 1990s, and again from 2004-2007 as director of promotions and community affairs for WDEF-FM and WDOD-FM.

When I first got my start in the radio broadcasting industry, Danny Howard, then WDEF program director and now operations manager, had placed a little plastic ear right in front of the audio board as a reminder to the DJs that he was listening. Whether or not he was listening that early in the morning I never knew, but someone was always listening, even if it did not feel like it in those early morning hours. My air shift was over at 6:00 in the morning and Luther showed up well before then to prepare for the WDEF morning show. I knew for sure people were listening then. People were waking up and preparing for the day while listening to Luther. Not having grown up in Chattanooga, I did not understand at that time Luther's significance to broadcasting and to his community, although that changed very quickly. I learned about both Luther's amazing career in broadcasting and his kindness. Here's just one example: every morning, he would enter the studio with a smile and a donut for me. I was always very appreciative that he thought of me. I would graciously smile and thank him as I accepted his kind gesture. One morning Luther walked in with his usual warm greeting. He just looked at me and said, "You don't like donuts, do you?" A bit embarrassed, I said, "Sir, I really appreciate your thoughtfulness toward me, but I...uh...," He interrupted and said, "It's okay." I quickly replied, "No, but I really appreciate how you think of me every morning. I really do." He just nodded his head and said, "Thank you for telling me." The next morning, and every morning thereafter until the last day I worked the overnight shift, Luther brought me a banana. Every morning. It was a seemingly simple gesture, but it was a thoughtful one. It meant a lot to know someone was thinking of you.

Luther is a considerate gentleman who has had an amazing career. I am honored to know him and have worked with him for so many years. Most of all I am honored to call him my friend, and now, a friend of my family. Both of my children's early vocabulary included the word "Lutha." I hold his words of wisdom close to my heart, especially in regards to family. On his 90th birthday, I was with James and Luther as they spoke to the UTC communication students on campus. While waiting for James to return, I asked Luther if he had any special advice on such a monumental day. With a few tears in his eyes, he adjusted his glasses and jokingly gave me a hard time for his uncharacteristic show of emotion. As he tucked his white hanky back in his jacket pocket, he told me to keep doing what I'm doing: "Continue to support your husband and to be with your children." With age comes wisdom, and I was honored to have shared that moment with him.

Luther, thank you for your friendship, kindness and encouragement. I am honored to have crossed your path in life.

Lee Hope
Television Director for CBS Chicago

Lee worked with Luther while he served as the director of News 12 This Morning and the audio operator of News 12 at Noon at WDEF-TV (June 1993-December 1996). He also worked at Sunny 92.3 part-time as a radio personality and remote producer (January 1994-July 1999).

Some of the things I appreciate most about Luther are his humor and generosity. It's the memories of constant joking and laughing that I will always remember. Whenever I talk to James, we always share a Luther story that makes us both laugh so much. One of the stories includes a time when, in the lobby at News12 and [then] Sunny 92.3 studios, I was paged to receive a visitor. It was a pretty young lady I knew named Emily from the Chattanooga Symphony who had stopped by to surprise me with some cookies. I was taken aback and was feeling pretty good about myself while standing there talking to her. Luther heard the page for me to come to the lobby and was watching me on the surveillance camera from the upstairs radio studio. I was just about to give Emily a quick tour of the station when Luther walked down the stairs and introduced himself. This made me feel even better about my chances of making a good impression on sweet Emily. Luther was very nice, telling her what a great guy and worker I was. Then, as Luther was heading back up the stairs, he turned around and used his oldest but best joke. He said, "Hey, Lee, by the way, the drug store just called. They said they don't have Preparation-H in two gallon drums." I will never forget how Emily looked at me as Luther proceeded back up the stairs to the radio studios. Truly a classic Luther moment!

Not only is Luther funny, he is extremely generous. I often gave him a ride to pick up his truck after News12 at Noon. During one of these times, my car was in the shop for a major repair. Luther found out about it and asked to go with me to the shop. When we got there, he paid for the repairs, over $600.

Luther, from your "ol' pal" Lee, thank you so much for your humor and generosity. I still share some of your jokes to this day!

Photo courtesy of WDEF-TV Archives

Chip Chapman and Luther.

Chip Chapman

Chip worked together with Luther in both television and radio. He did after-noons on WDEF-AM while Luther was doing mornings. Chip went to WDEF-TV full-time and anchored the morning and noon show. Luther was a big part of both of those broadcasts.

Luther's presence is larger than life. Whenever you do any sort of public appearance with Luther, you might as well just enjoy the ride. It's like being caught in a tidal wave. If you go somewhere with Luther, and of course it has been promoted on the air for a couple of weeks, there are dozens and dozens if not hundreds of people there. You think, "Wow, what a great event!" and it doesn't take you long to realize they are not there to see you; they are there to see Luther. It is always fun to go to public appearances like that with him. It doesn't matter if you are going to have lunch or a remote broadcast because the man will draw an audience.

I have known Luther for 35 years and have worked with hundreds of really great people in broadcasting. Without a doubt, Luther is the absolute most selfless. He always, and I mean always, puts the needs of other people before his own. I have never seen Luther put his own needs above someone else. This is just a small instance, but there were a number of charities that I used to be involved with, such as Special Olympics, Sudden Infant Death Syndrome Foundation, and several others over the years. One of the big things about charities is that you are doing fundraisers all the time. Luther would hear about it because we'd talk about it on the air, and he would come down to my little part of the studio. He would visit for a while – not too long because Luther doesn't stay in one place for very long – but we'd talk for a little while. He'd get up to leave and invariably there would be an envelope left there that would be made out to a specific charity. It would be a check or cash from Luther, with very distinctive handwriting that you could pick out from a hundred others. I would chase him down or thank him for it the next day, and he would just sort of shrug his shoulders. He was always giving like that. Those are just some of the cases that I know about, and I know there are hundreds – and I do mean hundreds – of other cases like that where Luther has made a very significant contribution, but he does it on the condition of anonymity. He doesn't want anybody to know. That's his Christian, charitable, giving spirit.

Not only is Luther charitable, he is a very kind and loyal man in both word and deed. That is quite a legacy to leave. Those of us who have worked with him over the years are lucky enough to consider ourselves part of his extended family, but the man has no equal when it comes to loyalty. Out of all the people that I have ever met in my life, I think Luther is the one that I have never heard anybody say a bad word about. I have never heard anyone say a bad word about Luther Masingill. I think that is quite a legend in itself.

Bobby Daniels

Bobby Daniels has worked in Chattanooga radio since 1988 at various radio stations. Since 1998, he has worked either full- or part-time at WDEF Sunny

92.3 with Luther. Bobby used to work the afternoon drive time slot at Sunny 92.3 full-time and continues to host a show there and work part-time on weekends.

Many of us see somebody on TV or hear someone on the radio and wonder what they are really like. When it comes to Luther, I know from personal experience that he is a man with a beautiful heart and a genuine love and concern for the people. He demonstrates that every day he comes in to work and every day he is on the air.

One year, it was getting close to Christmas and I was working on the air at WDEF. It was getting later in the day and Luther came by the radio station, as he often did, but I was a little surprised to see him at that time of the day. "Hey, Luther," I said, as we proceeded to share a few of the same jokes that we often did, like how he stays in such good shape every day because in the morning he touches the tips of his shoes a hundred times and then he takes them off the dresser and puts them on his feet. This particular evening, I was a bit more dressed up than usual, and Luther said, "What have you got going on tonight?" I told him that I had some family in from out of town and we were going to go to the Town and Country Restaurant for dinner one last time before it closed. Luther proceeded to go into his studio, which I can see through the glass, and he picked up the phone. He then came back into the studio and said, "Hey, I just thought I would come in before you go," and with his hand on the counter said, "Listen, when you go over to the Town and Country, ask for..." – and he gave me the name of a particular waitress – "and tell him that Luther sent you. You guys have a good Christmas. Merry Christmas." Luther turned to leave and there on the counter was a folded up 100 dollar bill. He bought our dinner that night, and the waitress Luther told us to ask for made certain we had a wonderful evening at the Town and Country Restaurant. Luther is that kind of guy.

Luther, I respect you as a broadcaster; I really do. What you have done and continue to do is nothing short of amazing, and I hope I can even come close in my chosen career field to match what you have done. I respect you as a broadcaster, but I appreciate and love you as a friend. You have been a father figure to me. You have shown me love and compassion, and you have shown me that people in this business, if they model themselves after you, they're going to be okay. God bless you, Luther.

Kevin Hayes
Overnight DJ, WDOD-FM

Kevin grew up listening and watching Luther on radio and television. He has worked with Luther for approximately 8 years.

The first time I met Luther was when I started working here in Chattanooga. I will say that I was in awe because I have been watching Luther since I was a child. I moved away and eventually returned to see that Luther was still on television and radio. I'll admit I was a little star-struck. I was working at another radio station within the Bahakel Group, WDOD. WDEF and WDOD were located in the same building, and so one morning, I decided I was going to meet Luther. I went in and said, "Hey, Luther, my name is Kevin. I work for 96.5 The Mountain. I just wanted to say hi and introduce myself to you." I did not want to bother him, and he looked really busy, but he actually turned around, looked at me and said, "Hey, it's nice to meet you, Son. I hope you have a great day." Ever since then, Luther and I have been good friends. I really admire Luther. He is a funny guy and someone I enjoy being around.

Luther, I really enjoy working with you. You have been a great inspiration for me as a young person coming up in radio.

Jeff Fontana
General Sales Manager, 1990-present, Radio Account Executive, 1987-1990

When I first started at WDEF Radio, I asked Luther how long he planned on working. At that time, it would have been his 46th year. He explained that "he would love to make it to 50 years." That was almost 25 years ago! Amazing. Of course I'd heard about Luther, and very early in my career, I had the chance to witness the "Luther and Snow" phenomenon. Chattanooga had a snow early in 1989, long before the internet, and that morning I'd made it in to help answer phone calls on Luther's morning show. It was pretty wild and impressive to say the least. I answered one call where the lady said that she wanted to let her employees know that she was closing because of the snow and ice on the roads. I asked her for the name of her business and how many employees she had. She told me the name of her business and that she had one employee. I said, "Don't you think it would be easier just to call your employee?" She laughed and said that she was the employee and just wanted to hear Luther say her company name on his show for all the publicity. I'm sure that she was not the only one that has done that over the years.

You knew that if Luther mentioned a snowstorm, bread and milk would fly off the shelves, but he also had a personal touch. Once, we were doing a remote broadcast at a local grocery store and Luther was present. There was a little boy who wanted to ride a pony on one of the small quarter rides. The little boy's mother was yelling, telling him "No!" Luther saw that the boy was quite unhappy and slipped him a dollar. He made that child's day.

Luther, you are one amazing person that has touched several generations in this region. God has put you on this earth to make sure that everyone that has lost a pet has now found it or to make sure that we have bread and milk before a snowstorm. Most importantly, God put you here because life would not be the same without waking up to hear that familiar voice on the radio.

THE CHATTANOOGA TIMES: CHATTANOO

The Waking-up Voice

—Times Staff Photo by W. C. King.

WILLIAM LUTHER MASINGILL

Image courtesy of WDEF-TV Archives

Luther Masingill, "The Waking-up Voice" of Chattanooga.

7

Luther on History and Values

Luther's career in broadcasting is unprecedented. He has earned many endearing titles over the years including the "Voice of Chattanooga." He has had a career like no other broadcaster in the history of the world. He is in his 72nd consecutive year on the air, with the same station, and is said to be the only radio personality to have reported both the Pearl Harbor and the 9/11 attacks on the United States.

I did not know about being the only broadcaster in history to have announced both Pearl Harbor and the 9/11 attacks. It was brought up by an out-of-town reporter who had heard about me and the longevity of my career. He asked about me being on duty on Pearl Harbor day and about some of the other events all down through history from then until now. "In fact, he has stayed on duty just about all the time," they'd say about me. But yes, I learned about it just a few years ago that I was one of the ones who happened to be on duty during these events.

With as long as Luther has been on the air and as much as he has seen and announced over the years, Luther has developed a sense of trust with his listeners. From history to snowflakes, Luther is a man that people have learned to trust as a source of information. The question has jokingly been asked, "What happens when you combine Luther and a snowflake?" When Luther mentions it is going to snow, everybody suddenly heads for the store for milk and bread. Luther's listeners have such faith in his pronouncements

209

that Luther has had to learn to carefully monitor his words. In 1979 when he talked about a possible gas shortage, listeners immediately flocked to area gas stations. My dad still talks about how, back in the '70s, Luther said, "Get your gas. Get it now due to the possibility of a shortage." Just Luther mentioning the possibility was almost enough to cause an actual shortage of gas!

When I made the comment about a possible gas shortage, it was not in a hectic or hysterical way. It was simply a comment. I'd mentioned very casually that there might be a gas shortage and I would get some to keep from running out when going to work or taking the kids to school. I just kind of casually mentioned it and it grew out of that. People ran to the stations to get gas just so they wouldn't run out. It did cause a little consternation and a little concern. I did not want to make people inconvenience the service stations or the gas company or anything, but it did kind of help. The people got the gas in their car and they were ready for any emergency. If I remember correctly, it did not turn out as bad as they thought. I think my manager may have said something to me. "Hey, be careful. Watch that. You've got a good following and they depend on you. If you tell them it is going to snow, they buy out all the bread and milk at the stores. You have quite a bit of influence, and just mentioning a shortage of gas, it might present a problem. Be careful," he told me. "Okay," I said. "I'll be careful. Thank you and have a nice day."

Luther has witnessed and announced so much history throughout his career, from the attack of Pearl Harbor on December 7, 1941, to the World Trade Center situation – the terrorist attacks on September 11, 2001. I asked Luther to describe what it was like as a broadcaster the day that the Japanese attacked Pearl Harbor, the day that Franklin Delano Roosevelt described as a "date which will live in infamy."

It was a very quiet Sunday afternoon. I was on duty as a young boy, still going to high school. I had the afternoon shift, and as I said, it was just very quiet. A religious program had just gone off the air when I heard the bell ringing. Back in those days, you had a news machine that kind of looked like a typewriter. It was electronically controlled from wherever the news was coming from and it started ringing. It was ringing and ringing and it just kept getting faster. By this time it was ringing frantically, and I knew I had a news bulletin. I immediately ran down the hall and tore it off. It said, "THE JAPANESE HAVE ATTACKED THE ISLAND OF OAHU!" That did not mean much to me as a young man. I had never been to Hawaii, and back in those days, there were a lot of things like that happening around the world. In other words, I did not realize the significance of it. I really did not, but I read it. And I waited for the next bell to ring, which was just about five minutes later. There was another series of bells ringing with a follow up. The follow up had the approximate number of planes that had attacked Pearl Harbor, along with some additional information. It was a quiet Sunday afternoon until that moment when the bulletin came over. Boy, it sure did start moving from then on. It was hectic with the amount of news that people wanted and we had to give it to them. Normally, the weekends were slow when it came to news, especially on Sunday afternoons, but when that bulletin came in and the following one and all the others that followed, it was a busy, busy place. Staff members that worked during the week came in, and it was just something. I don't think we got the number of deaths verified for two or three days, but let me tell you — Pearl Harbor — I remember it.

Photo courtesy of WDEF-TV Archives

Luther (right) as a young man monitoring and reading the news bulletins.

Like so many other Americans, I will never forget September 11, 2001. My family was planning a vacation to Gulf Shores, Alabama. I had my father-in-law's truck and in the back was a sailboat. That morning, Christy and Gracie were going to meet me in the parking lot of the radio station here on South Broad Street. We were going to drive to Gulf Shores and spend the week with family, just relaxing, sailing and skiing. It was 8:30 a.m. and my duties on the morning show were pretty much finished. I was hanging around, talking with Luther and the late Parker Smith, while waiting for my family to show up so we could leave for Gulf Shores. Parker was working by himself that morning on WDOD. He had pretty much wrapped up his show, and music was playing as we were talking. I was leaning against the counter in the WDOD studio and the television above Parker's head was on mute. We were talking, and I remember how I felt that day. I was relaxed, the sun was shining, and we were about to leave for a week of vacation. It was just a nice morning and I was feeling really good when suddenly Parker looked up and said, "Oh man! It looks like the World Trade Center is on fire! Is that live? It looks like the Trade Center is on fire!" Instantly my mood changed as I looked up and then ran straight to the AP wire. We subscribe to the Associated Press, and I ripped off a script. At the time it just said, "A fire with possible entrapment in the World Trade Center in New York City."

I walked in my studio and tapped on Luther's window. Luther looked up, "Yes, James? What have you got?" I nervously pointed to his screen, "Look at your television. They are talking about the World Trade Center being on fire." I continued to read the scripts about what was taking place in New York City. At that time, no one really knew an airliner had crashed into it. Then rumors began to emerge that an airplane had hit the World Trade Center. As reports were coming in and we were trying to confirm information, we continued to go live on the air. Luther started reminiscing about a B-25 Mitchell bomber that crashed into the Empire State Building back in 1945, an accident caused by heavy fog. As he was talking on the radio, the AP was just going nuts on my computer. I would click on the computer while we were talking, and more information kept coming in, until it was finally confirmed that an airplane had slammed into the World Trade Center. Obviously, all the networks were covering the event, and it did not take long before we realized what was happening. We had gone to a commercial break, came out of it, and were playing a Kenny G song. We were watching network coverage when suddenly another airplane hit. "Oh my, another airplane just hit the World Trade Center! This is crazy," I said. "Fade out of this song. We've got to get on the air now!" To this day I still get chills just thinking about it. From that point on, we went wall-to-wall coverage with CBS News. We were talking about it live for maybe an hour or an hour and a half, reading the reports and relaying the information we had to the public. I remember asking someone to make sure I was pronouncing Osama bin Laden correctly. "Am I saying that right? Osama bin Laden?" I asked one of the guys in the studio as I pointed to his name on the report. "Is this how you pronounce his name?" I hate to even say this, but most everyone knows how to pronounce his name now.

My family eventually showed up at the station, and of course they had been listening, but they did not understand what was going on either. "I cannot go to Gulf Shores right now," I said. Everyone was on edge and the media hype was enormous. Nobody really knew what to think or how to feel. I remember talking to Chattanooga Tower employees and questioning their safety. We also interviewed the staff at Blood Assurance because they were gearing up for a potential disaster. "We need to store up blood. This could be World War III," they said. The atmosphere was unbelievable. It was all very disconcerting. I worked more than 17 hours on September 11, 2001, and we continued wall-to-wall coverage with CBS news for the next couple days. I went to talk to our general manager at the time, Gary Downs. He said, "Hey listen, we are going to play some music and we are going to stick with network coverage for a while. Go on vacation. Get with your family." I had a difficult time with his advice, but knew I could not do much else at the time. Here is how Luther remembers that day:

Oh, what a mess that day was! We were working our shifts on 9/11. I was reading radio copy when the first plane collided, so I did not actually see when the first plane crashed into the World Trade Center. I was in the studio when I saw the second plane hit the other building and that was something. There was all that smoke, and of course, the hope that people would get out safely. I remember there was a man they were showing on television, a man who was sitting on the steps of a building close by. As you were seeing the plane head right toward the building, he was not looking at it. But, as it hit the building, he looked up and the expression on his face was one of horror, of "hey, this cannot be true – two buildings, two planes – all those people are going to be killed if they don't get out of the building", and of course, a lot of them never did as you well know.

It reminded me of a time in the '40s when a military plane, a B-25 Mitchell bomber, crashed into the Empire State Building. There were a number of people killed, but it sure did not bring down the building. On 9/11, when the first plane hit the first of the two buildings, everybody for quite a few minutes thought it was a small plane similar to what you fly when you go out in a plane with your family or friends. That's what they thought it was, but after closer inspection and some close-up views by the television cameras, you could see it wasn't. From the measurement of the building where that plane went in, the first one, it sure wasn't a small plane. It was a big one going at a high rate of speed and it was heavy enough to break its way into that building. What a mess that day was...a sad day for our country.

When 9/11 took place, I was a part of the Coast Guard Auxiliary. I had tried getting into the military but was not accepted due to a football injury and having three pins in my knee. Yet on 9/11, more so than on any other day in my life, I just knew that I wanted to do something for my country. I wanted to go over there and fight. I wanted to get in line and sign up and fight whoever caused this grief and this pain to my country. One day during that week at Gulf Shores, I sat on a pier and watched a group of Navy planes go back and forth in what looked like some type of training exercise. As I sat there watching, I began to reflect on why I had entered the Coast Guard Auxiliary. At the time, I was a vessel examiner in the Coast Guard, but the whole reason I entered the Coast Guard Auxiliary was to be a pilot in their pilot program. That week is when I decided I would start studying to be a part of the search-and-rescue patrol, called the MET Patrol, the acronym for the Marine Environmental Patrol. I set my goal and decided to start studying for those tests. I decided that week that I was going to do something when it came to the military and serving my country. I was very depressed that week due to the loss of life and the tragedy of 9/11. It was a sad day for so many Americans and truly a somber week that changed the course of American history.

Photo by Holly Abernathy

Images of the Twin Towers at the World Trade Center complex taped to a pole outside of FDNY Engine Company 10 and FDNY Ladder Company 10 across from Ground Zero. New York, New York.
"We Will Always Remember."

When tragedy strikes, such as events like Pearl Harbor or 9/11, I think we all generally remember where we were in life. Luther has talked about a few specific dates in history where he remembers exactly where he was and what he was doing. Luther describes the day when President John F. Kennedy was assassinated in Dallas, Texas:

It was November 22, 1963. I was on duty in the broadcast studio of WDEF on Broad Street down when we were in the same building with WDEF Channel 12 television. In fact, I was having lunch there at the station. The bulletin came in that there was a shooting. That's the way they described it first. I don't remember the exact text of it, but that's quite a shocker when you hear that your President is on the receiving end of a rifle shot in Dallas, Texas. It kind of scares you and you wait very impatiently for the next bulletin. The next one came a few seconds later and said "JFK has been hit." The governor had reportedly been hit also, but Mrs. Kennedy had not been hit. All we could do was read the remarks of our own government officials who weren't sure he was dead. It took a while, but they finally made the announcement that the President was dead. I remember Walter Cronkite's rather emotional delivery of the news. He had to swallow a couple times before he could really clear his throat and say, "From Dallas, Texas, the flash apparently official, President Kennedy died at 1:00 p.m. central standard time, 2:00 o'clock eastern standard time, some 38 minutes ago." For so many people, that's how they received the message. It was a memorable day. It changed the headlines of every newspaper in the world when that happened.

All my life, I have been fascinated with the space program. I have seen clip after clip of Walter Cronkite's coverage of the space endeavors of the United States, including the Apollo and the Mercury missions, the astronauts, and of course, the first man on the moon, Neil Armstrong. Although it was before I was born, I later watched the clips and remember listening to Neil Armstrong, after putting his left foot down on the moon, say, "That's one small step for man, one giant leap for mankind." I tried to imagine what it was like for Neil Armstrong and Edwin "Buzz" Aldrin to be the first men to ever step foot on the moon, while astronaut and third member of the crew, Michael Collins, fretted about their safe return to the mothership, *Columbia.* I also wondered what it was like for Americans to be watching that day. These three men made history on July 20, 1969. Sadly, we lost Neil Armstrong this year when he died on August 25, 2012. He was 82 years old. I often wondered what it was like for Luther when Neil Armstrong first stepped on the moon.

The whole world was watching that day and we were too. Some have jokingly asked over the years if we had a "moon party" complete with Moon Pies and RC Cola or Nehi Grape. No, we did not. We were just watching like everyone else. It was very quiet, although we had some neighbors over and some relatives were in town, but we witnessed it just like everybody else. We were so glad when they landed safely and Neil Armstrong walked down that ladder. There was no doubt in my mind that it was real. Some people would say, "Well, they are not up there really. That's out west somewhere in a mountainous area," but I believed that they were. I believed they were accomplishing what they set out to do. After the excitement of it all, I would recall so many things that caught my attention, like the dust on the moon. I would always hope when they went back to the moon again that they would land somewhere close to where they did before, so we could closely examine what was left there on previous trips. It would have been interesting to see what the extreme temperatures did to the things they'd left on the moon. But yes, the whole world was watching that day and so were we here in Chattanooga.

Photo courtesy of WDEF-TV Archives

Luther in the early 1960s.

Luther has lived a rich and long life, 90 years and counting. You cannot live that long without learning a few important lessons that really stick with you. I wanted to know what those lessons were, and what Luther has learned over his many years. I wanted to glean from his life experiences and take whatever wisdom he was willing to share with me. Over the years, I have had the opportunity to learn who Luther is through everyday conversation and simply by living so much of my life with Luther. When you work side-by-side with someone every day for so long, you really get to know that person. I had specific questions I wanted to ask him. I wanted to understand his sense of values and how that had developed throughout the course of his life. He has been a witness, through the medium of broadcasting, to some of the most significant events in history. He has seen life and death, and he has been through love and loss. He has experienced a long life and has watched the world change one decade at a time.

I am very sentimental about death and things, the death of a loved one. I was around when President Roosevelt died and I remember watching the people off to the side, watching the funeral procession. They were brought to tears with his passing. I also remember tears coming to my eyes during the funeral procession of President Kennedy. You mourn great people and their passing, and tears come to your eyes, especially with the sound of a certain piece of music during the funeral or the procession. The person means so much, whether it's your leader, your friend, or your relative; you mourn them and their passing.

I saw death in the service during World War II, serving in New Guinea and in the Admiralty Islands and down in Australia for a while. That's where we landed and did some training. Death will kind of shake you up. If you ever see a person draw his or her last breath, it's something you remember for a long time, especially if it's somebody you love. I remember when Mom died, which was later than Dad of course, but a loved one's death will shake you. When my father died, I was just a teenager. I was right out of high school. Even when he was so close to death, I know Daddy was hoping we would continue with our sense of humor because even then he would try to pull a joke or something that would tickle us or please us. He went very quietly and without pain, and we missed him so much. Even still, it was good that we could all retain our sense of humor because I believe that's the way Daddy wanted it. I also believe that if you've been saved and believe in Jesus Christ and live a good life, I believe you'll go to heaven when you die. Those are my beliefs and I'll believe them until I die, and I better see you up there in heaven, James, or you're going to be in a lot of trouble. I'm going to haunt you! {Laughs}

Luther has been married for 55 years and counting. His views on marriage are very traditional. As time goes on, more and more couples are choosing to live together rather than get married. When Luther got married, "living together" wasn't really seen as an option. I asked Luther to describe his views and beliefs on love and marriage.

Love...well, you've got to have it. If you don't, chaos, that's what you'll have. Mary and I have been married for 55 years. To me, love is seeing how happy you can make the other person. You try to make them as happy as you can. That's my philosophy, to try to be as good to them as you can. They in turn will do the same for you in most cases. I think marriage is a two-way proposition; you've got to give and the other person has to give. You've got to put up with some of the things that aggravate you in your partner, and they in turn have to do the same. That way you get to know each other better and you get along better over a period of time. People nowadays, they want to live together a while and see if it works out. I cannot see that. It doesn't sound right and a lot of times it doesn't work out too well.

Just be sure you got the right gal, with the right morals. Be sure she has some morals. It's good if you can find someone in a church or if she found you in a church. That was our situation, and it helps when you've got some religious training behind you and inside of you. I would suggest you just be careful about the person you choose. Be sure they have some morals and understand that it's about "doing unto others, the things you'd like done unto you." Love is just trying to live with somebody, being good to them, and both of you doing your best to make each other happy. That's very important.

Photo courtesy of David Carroll

Luther and Mary Masingill in Chicago, November 2012.

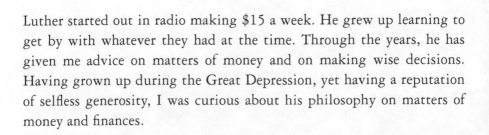

Luther started out in radio making $15 a week. He grew up learning to get by with whatever they had at the time. Through the years, he has given me advice on matters of money and on making wise decisions. Having grown up during the Great Depression, yet having a reputation of selfless generosity, I was curious about his philosophy on matters of money and finances.

Keep it. Don't give it away {laughs}. No, no. Remember your church and your loved ones and their needs. Provide what you can to meet their needs and let them live a normal life. I was never known as a stingy person, not that I know of, and I did not make very much starting out in this business in radio. It was 15 dollars a week. You did not make very much as a part-time apprentice announcer, still in high school.

Earlier on, during the Great Depression, you lived with what you had. Your breakfast was gravy and a biscuit. You very seldom had meat like bacon or sausage or something like that. Once in a while, you might have some. But you really did not know you were poor. You were poor, but you did not make a big to-do of it. You weren't being compared to the richest people in your city or anything like that. As young kids growing up, Daddy worked hard and he brought home a salary. I don't know how much. I don't have any idea, but occasionally, because as a drummer he called on stores, he would find a bargain on some apples, oranges, or bananas. He loved to bring home bananas. We all loved bananas, so if he found a bargain some-where and if he had the money for it, he would get a big sack of bananas. It always put a smile on our faces when he came in with something like that because we just weren't used to it. Being poor wasn't too bad really. I think the hardest times were being poor in the wintertime when you did not have enough money to heat your house real well. At night, you would go to bed and Mom and Daddy put so many covers on you that you couldn't turn over. You just had to stay right where you were all night. When we woke up, we would head to either the kitchen or the dining room where we usually had a coal-burning or wood-burning stove. So being poor wasn't too bad. We had a lovely family and we had a good momma and daddy who provided for us.

Now, I like to pay my bills on time. I don't like to owe money. If I assume a debt, I like to pay it off as quickly as possible and do it without sacrificing other necessities. I try to be sensible. I just try to use good common sense in terms of money or the transaction of money.

Finally, I asked Luther his thoughts on education and the value he puts on education. Having been in the same business for the last 70 years, he is an authority in the field of broadcasting. The industry Luther made history in has changed so much over the years, and technology has changed the way we receive information. What if someone wanted to get into the career of broadcasting today? I wanted to know if Luther, having been in the business for so long and having seen so many changes over the years, would still advise someone to get into the field of broadcasting today.

If you're going to get in it, get in it and work hard. You need to study and read a lot. That's what they always told me. My speech teacher in high school asked, "You're really interested in this radio thing, aren't you, Luther?" "Yes, sort of," I said. I met her one time at a teacher's meeting, and she told me to read and read a lot. "Read your newspapers, read magazines, pick out good books and read them. You'd be surprised at how much it broadens your mind. Read, read, read, Luther. Do that. Keep up with what's going on right now, this morning, tonight. Keep up with what's going on. Be informed so that you can answer any question anybody ever asks you about the city, about the county, about the state, about your business and about how much you like radio and television broadcasting," she advised.

It was good advice. I'm all for education. Get as much of it as you can and don't bypass the opportunity. If you get a chance to go to college, go. If you cannot, try to study something, try to learn something. Learn as much as you can. I'm in a business where I learn every day. In this business of television and radio, you learn something new every day. You're kept up-to-date with what's going on in the world. Understand that if you do go into this business, you're not going to make a great deal of money. You're not going to get rich right away. It's a long, drawn-out thing. Being local may lead into something national and that's where the money is, in national broadcasting. The big money is with the networks and cable. I never saw so many stations. I believe if you ask me about getting into this business, I would say go ahead and get in it and give it a try. If you don't like it and if you're not suitable for it, get your hind end out of it!

As for me, I'm just grateful Joe Engel gave me my start as a public address announcer at his ballpark, Engel stadium. When he opened WDEF, I asked him for a job and he gave me one. I've been in radio and television ever since.

Photo courtesy of WDEF-TV Archives

Luther at the beginning of his broadcasting career at the WDEF studios.

Photo by Daisy Moffatt

Luther, still on the air, at the WDEF studios in September 2012.

8
Luther's Legacy

At some point in our lives, most of us will stop and ask ourselves what our legacy will be, wondering what we will leave behind when our life ceases to exist. In certain moments, we reflect on what we have done and what we have accomplished in life. We question if our achievements, whatever they may be, will survive the test of time and live beyond the vapor of our existence. In these thoughtful moments, we question if we have lived our life well and if what we have done will continue to live on even when our life has ended. We question the meaning and purpose of our lives, and we hope to see, reflected in our thoughts, a life well lived.

I love Luther and I pray he has many more years of life on this earth. Like so many others, I consider myself blessed to be a part of his life. I believe when the time comes, he will leave a legacy of love, compassion and generosity to his family and friends, to Chattanooga, and to the broadcasting industry. I believe he has left a mark on his profession that is unmatched by any other broadcaster in history. He is a man from humble beginnings, yet his professional and moral consistency in life has led him down a road that has made history unachieved by any other. Luther has lived a life that he and those he loves can be proud of, and so often we think of those we love first when reflecting on our life and the legacy we will leave behind.

Sometimes I think about Momma and Daddy. I think about what I might tell them or ask them if they were here. I might ask, "Mom and Dad, how'd I turn out? Here I am in the broadcasting business. People know me. I work with some good guys. I always wonder, what do you think? How did we do? How have we done with our families and with our jobs and with our association with our fellow Chattanoogans? What do you think now, Momma and Dad, after you see us?"

I also think of my own children. Two of the greatest moments of my life were the births of both of my children, Jeffrey and Joan. I remember looking at them and thinking, "Gee whiz, healthy, all ten toes, all ten fingers and everything is working and working right." That, I think, is an accomplishment and you're so grateful. I married late in my life, and you worry about things that can happen to an offspring at a later age. I was only in my 30s, but I always felt that I should have gone ahead and married at an earlier age and had a child when we were 20 or 21, but they turned out to be – both of them – good as gold and I love them and would do anything for them.

I wish now, though, that I'd spent a little more time or took a little more time off from my work. I love my work so much, but of course I love my children and my wife, Mary. I do look back and I could've taken some more time off. We could've gone somewhere with them. I'd love to have seen Yosemite. They always wanted to see Yosemite, but we went to a lot of different places over the country. I wish we had traveled more, but you go through life and you do your best.

Some of Jeffrey and Joanie's fondest memories of their dad include the personal time he spent with them. Joanie says she shares so many fond memories with her dad, but one she remembers in particular: "We used to drive down to Florida almost every year for a vacation. We were at the motel and I wanted to jump off the diving board, but I was too afraid to do it. So my dad stood there on the side of the pool and held my hand as I jumped off the side of the diving board. I must have done it a hundred times, but every time he held my hand. Of course he was soaking wet by the time we were finished, and I don't know if I ever went off the end of the board. I just kept going off the side, but I was happy and he was there until I got tired of doing it. It sounds so insignificant, but it meant a lot to me.

I have a lot of fond memories and I'm very proud of my dad. I'm probably the most proud of the kind of person that he is and the way he cares about others. I never hear my dad say anything bad about anybody. He just doesn't talk bad about people. He is always trying to find the good in things and in people. Sure, he has won a lot of great awards and we are always proud of him for those things, but that is really not what defines him to me."

Luther shared the following with me regarding his view of children:

Be good to your children and listen to them. A lot of parents won't listen to their children. If they've got a story to tell, sit down and listen to them and try to help them. It's important to listen and to avoid harsh discipline. I always thought harsh discipline was unnecessary. If you could get your point across some other way, do it the other way without that type of punishment.

I'm 90 years old and I've seen a lot. I've seen a lot of mistreatment of children, a lot of being hateful to children by parents. It always hurt me to see a child hurt. When you see the feelings of a child hurt, you want to say, "Hey, Fellow, I know you're his daddy, but don't do that." If you know him well enough, you can do that, but if you don't, you better keep your mouth shut and let them work it out some other way. Sometimes when you're in a position such as a radio announcer, you can get away with it, but I just love and appreciate parents who are respectful of their children. I always tried to be that way with my own children, and I love them and I would do anything for them.

Luther and Mary's marriage has inspired me ever since I got to know Luther and his family. When I first started at WDEF, I would come in an hour before my air shift and just sit and talk with him. The more I got to know him and understand what his values were and the relationship that he and Mary had, the more I wanted my young marriage to resemble the success of Luther's marriage. I wanted a relationship like Luther and Mary. I knew it wasn't perfect, yet they worked through the challenges and I wanted to model that in my own marriage. Anyone who has been married knows you will experience hardship and struggles, but you get through it. You deal with it; you don't quit. I saw that in Luther and Mary and in their 55 years of marriage. Luther has given me some great advice over the years. His guidance has included teaching me the importance of two simple phrases: "I'm sorry" and "I love you." People in Luther's generation weren't big on saying those words. You just did not hear them much back when he was young, and you can tell it is difficult for him to say them. So when he speaks the words "I'm sorry" and "I love you," you know he definitely means it. I know when he gives this advice, he is sharing the wisdom and experience he's gained over the years and that these two phrases are a crucial part of any successful relationship.

There are things that are going to aggravate both of you. Put up with them until you get used to them or sit down and try to talk them out. You have to just tell them how you feel about being yelled at if you were yelled at, or if you were completely disregarded on a decision. Tell them how you feel. A lot of times that will smooth things out, if you are able to explain yourself. Above all, if you've hurt somebody in your family, your wife or your husband, apologize. That's the most magical thing in the world, the words "I'm sorry." Just say, "I'm sorry, I did not mean to do that, and I'll try not to do that again." You'd be surprised at how many things it can smooth over in a marriage. When you say something that hurts each other, before you go to bed that night, tell them you're sorry and try not to let it happen again. Those were the most magical words in our marriage. They smoothed everything out that was unpleasant.

I believe marriage and family is the greatest thing in the world, and what worries me about this country is the breakdown of the family. You've heard other people speak on this, learned men and women who worry about our country and the bringing up of our children. You hear how the parents are much less involved with their children and how this has an effect on their lives later on. I'd love to see our young people, our parents, go to church with their children and keep them active in the church. I believe it will help them end up with a more decent outlook on life and a greater sweetness toward their fellow man.

Every year, Luther and I would go to a local grocery store around the holidays to raise awareness for hunger. We would bag groceries for a couple hours to promote donations to the Chattanooga Food Bank and the Community Kitchen. One evening, we were at one of the grocery stores in a more affluent part of town, and Luther and I were bagging groceries. I asked the next patron if she wanted paper or plastic, and she glanced at me and coldly replied, "Paper!" I bagged her groceries while she continued to be rude and condescending toward me. Then, I put something in the wrong bag, and she said, "No, no! This goes right here." She was obviously aggravated with me but continued to talk to Luther. You could tell that talking to him was the highlight of her day. Luther was beginning to catch on to how she was treating me. While I was bagging the groceries, I was talking to Luther as well. She began to get perturbed because I was talking to him; she obviously thought I was an employee at the grocery store. After she paid for her groceries, Luther and I went outside with her to load the bags into the car. After I put her groceries in the trunk, Luther said, "By the way, I want you to meet my sidekick, James Howard." The look on her face was one of embarrassment, and you could tell she wanted to apologize for the way she had acted. It felt good when Luther did that. I did not care if he had mentioned my name or not, but it felt good. Luther did not like the way I had been treated and he made a point to let the woman know kindly that I was his "sidekick," his cohort. That's the kind of friend and the kind of person Luther is to people.

I've tried to be a good friend over the years. The thing I always avoided was hurting somebody's feelings. That's the worst thing in the world, to hurt someone with something you've said or done. I've always avoided reference to weight or looks. I remember feeling sorry for a little boy in grammar school. Bless his heart, he just wasn't attractive at all and the other children, as they will, made fun of him. I tried to befriend him in different ways and he seemed to appreciate it. In later years, I ran into him and he said, "I remember you and the kind words you gave me," as opposed to what other children said to him about his looks. Interestingly, he grew up and he wasn't a bad-looking guy at all, but when he was a kid, they would call him ugly. I did not ever say that of course, but friendship is a really important thing in life. You've got to have it. You got to have a good neighbor who will look after your house when you're gone. He's your burglar alarm. You got to have good relatives who will love you and who will respect you. You've got to have people you can sometimes call on, and you, in turn, can call on them, depending on what's going on in your life. Yes, you got to have friendship with a guy at the supermarket or the fellow you work with, and you've got to have respect for that person too. There are many reasons, but they are always there when you need them, and you're always there when they need you. You're crazy as a loon, James, but you're a good friend. I've had some good friends over the years. I've mentioned Buddy Houts several times. Of course my wife Mary, she's a good gal, a good gal. She's stuck with me all these years through this crazy radio and television business, but I believe she's enjoyed the relationship. I know I have and I love her very much.

For as long as I can remember, I have watched how Luther communicates with his audience. He has been on the air for more than 70 years. People know Luther not only as a radio guy; people know him as their friend, a relative, as a kind of father figure they have listened to all their lives. I have heard people relate to Luther in that way many times. Not too long ago, I heard a story about a guy from Washington, D.C. who married a girl from Chattanooga. They were married a little over 30 years ago here, and he remembers listening to Luther on the radio at the time. Shortly after they were married, he and his new bride moved back up to Washington, D.C. They lived there for a little over 30 years and, of course during that time, had not listened to Luther on the radio. The gentleman's wife has since passed away and he was visiting Chattanooga not too long ago. He turned on the radio and there was Luther, still on the air, just as he had been so many years ago as the man was beginning his life with his new bride. He recalled listening to Luther more than 30 years ago and asking his wife, "Who is this guy on the radio, helping people find their lost pets?" His wife answered him by saying, "It's Luther. Everybody knows who Luther is." Just in that brief time of listening to Luther — as a newlywed and then again when he returned to Chattanooga many years later — Luther made an impact on his life. The power of Luther's voice and his consistent presence on the air for so many years had the power to elicit personal memories from this man. Luther has done this from the beginning. He has impacted the hearts and minds of people over the span of many decades. He has helped out thousands of people in various ways over the course of his career. I admire the way Luther lives his life, both personally and professionally.

He has taught me what it means to be a broadcaster and to truly be a servant of my community. The greatest industry lesson Luther has ever taught me is to use broadcasting as a vehicle to help others. I've seen the old pictures of Luther playing such an active role in the community, from visiting hospitals to serving as a board member for numerous non-profit organizations. I have been by his side while he continues to serve year after year. I learned how to serve my community from him.

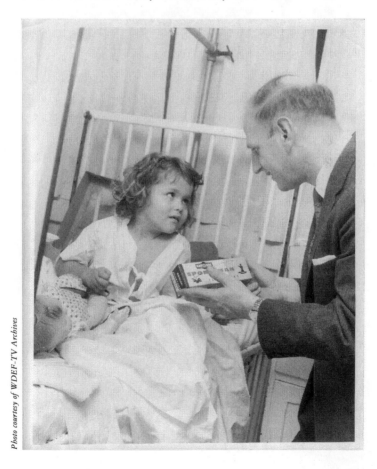

Photo courtesy of WDEF-TV Archives

Luther presents a gift to a child at the local children's hospital.

Photo courtesy of WDEF-TV Archives

Luther visits the local children's hospital during the holidays
in the early 1960s.

PTAs Make Luther Life Member

'LIFE' FOR LUTHER—Luther Masingill receives his life membership in the PTA from leaders of the group. From left, Mrs. Floyd Britton, Hamilton County PTA Council; Mr. Masingill, Mrs. Ross Russell, chairman of life membership committee; Mrs. Jack Vandergriff, chairman of school education.—(Staff Photo by Bill Truex.)

Luther receives his life membership in the Tennessee Congress of Parents and Teachers for community service, November 1963.

Luther handing out gifts at a community service event.

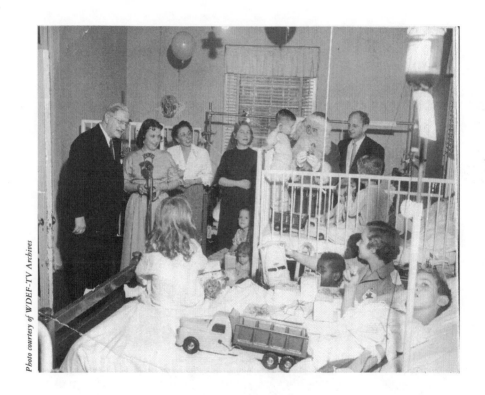

Photo courtesy of WDEF-TV Archives

Luther visits the local children's hospital during the Christmas season.

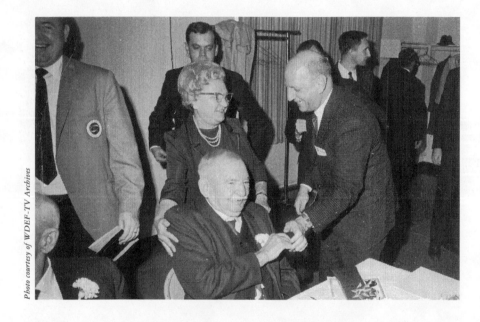

Photo courtesy of WDEF-TV Archives

Luther honors long standing community members during a service event.

Photo courtesy of WDEF-TV Archives

Luther on one of many visits to the local children's hospital in the late 1950s.

Image courtesy of WDEF-TV Archives

HEART ASSOCIATION OFFICIALS — New board members of the Chattanooga Area Heart Association were special guests at the executive committee meeting recently.
In front is Luther Masingill, Heart Sunday chairman. Behind him are Richard Robinson, left, and R.S. Mathews, chairman of the board. In the rear are Ben O. Gibbs, 1976 General Heart Fund chairman, left, and Patrick Crowe Jr. Mr. Crowe and Mr. Robinson are among the new board members. (Staff photo by Michael Crawford)

The board members (Luther front) of the Chattanooga Heart Association.

Image courtesy of WDEF-TV Archives

Heart Fund Chairman Masingill Urges Citizens Give Generously This Weekend

HEART SUNDAY TOMMOROW--Children at the Senter School help Heart Sunday Chairman Luther Masingill blow up reminders that it is time once again for Heart Volunteers to ask for contributions to aid in the fight against heart disease. From left are Tracie Perrin, Mr. Masingill, Johanna Kosik, Jeannie Masingill and Col. Parker.--(Staff color photo by John Shackleford.)

Heart Fund Chairman Luther Masingill during a community event urging citizens to give generously to aid in the fight against heart disease.

Some of my best days in radio have been when I was helping someone. I especially enjoyed working with Luther and the entire WDEF Radio staff to raise an average of $112,000 a year for T.C. Thompson's Children's Hospital. The whole reason I wanted to get into broadcasting is to help other people. Being able to help someone is another reason I am so passionate about doing traffic. Radio executives or industry professionals often discount the role of a traffic reporter, but it is not that way for me. As a traffic reporter, I feel like I am assisting someone in their commute to work. That is why I continue to do it. I love doing traffic and I love being part of the show in that role. It is doing what Luther taught me; it is helping people.

Another way we serve our community is by doing radio-a-thons. The four days a year that we are on the air raising money for kids with cancer are just wonderful. Many may not realize the preparation that is involved in these radio-a-thons; it involves months and months of work. We sit down with the parents and the children, and we listen to their stories. We spend a lot of time conducting interviews and attempting to convey to the listening audience how cancer impacts the lives of these children and their families. Those days, plus the time leading up to the radio-a-thons, are so fulfilling because you feel like you are doing something for someone. You are raising money while you are on the air and every dime is pumped back in – not to pay somebody's salary – but to go straight to the children and local families affected by cancer.

I have also tried to follow Luther's example of community service in my own way by visiting our local troops in the Middle East. When I went over to Iraq, Afghanistan and Jordan during the holidays, I hoped I was serving my community. I have broadcasted from the Middle East since 2004 and I plan on returning as long as the opportunity is available. I remember preparing for my first trip to Iraq. We took a banner to a local mall in Chattanooga and asked people to sign it with encouraging words so I could deliver it to the troops. An elderly lady came up to me and shook my hand, not knowing who I was at the time. She had tears in her eyes and she said, "I want you to tell James Howard that I think he is a hero and I just love him to death for doing this for our troops, for our boys." Tears welled up in her eyes and that made me tear up. She said, "Can you make sure to tell James that?" I just nodded my head and told her I would. I never did tell her I was James because it was just one of those moments where I did not feel like it was necessary. I felt like the message was more important than the messenger. Watching Luther and his career has helped me understand the importance of that, and to be a servant of my community and those around me.

When I entered Central High School, a man named Professor Nelson pulled me aside. He said, "I'm going to give you a little advice coming into Central High. I'm the principal, and if you step out of line, you're going to hear from me, in my office. Now, here's a little bit of advice. If you'll remember this, it'll help you in life. Do what's right because it's right and not because you're compelled to do it." That stayed with me. In fact, years later I ran into him at a cafeteria downtown and he remembered me. Of course, I'd been in his office several times for misbehaving {laughs}, but I mentioned to him that what he had said stuck with me all these years. Tears came to his eyes. He was very touched by that. When someone affects your life and you remember it, it really means a lot to that person that something they said had an effect on your life. Over the years, I've tried to put that into practice and always try to find a way to help someone if I am able. And it's the nicest compliment when someone walks up to you and recognizes you for it. Having done this for more than 70 years, you learn to read expressions. When they come out with "I love you. Can I hug you?", I always say, "Oh shoot, yeah, you can hug me! I never pass up a hug." It's that kind of thing that is a great reward. It means a lot when people remember you kindly because of something you found for them, or you helped them when their home was burned, or you found their lost dog or cat.

Occasionally, I'll do things like stop and cut the grass of a local business. I've been known to do things like that. Some people will see me out there doing that and say, "That guy is crazy. He's as crazy as a loon. He doesn't sound that way on the air, but he's crazy. That's not his grass!" You hear stuff like that, but many of them are appreciative. Buddy used to drive by and see me doing stuff like that sometimes. He'd say, "Nice going, Luther. Nice going," and drive off. There are so many ways you can help people, different ways, and there's a lot of ways you can help a person out on the air and they never forget it. They remember it forever.

Photo courtesy of WDEF-TV Archives

Luther has been known to carry lawn care equipment in the back of his truck
so he can tend to overgrown grass or weeds, wherever he spots them. One
restaurant owner even reported him "trimming their grass simply because it
needed it. He does not do it for thanks or any other reason. He just does it,
gets in his truck and goes on."

The radio business has changed so much with the boom in technology over
the last 20 years. The way people get their information has changed. At one
time, radio was the only medium where you could learn what was going
on in the world. Luther was there at the beginning when WDEF Radio
began. He was there at the inception of WDEF Television. For many years,
Luther was Chattanooga's main source of information. Even as the times
have changed and as Luther has aged, he has performed the amazing feat of

holding the same time slot at the same station longer than any other broadcaster in history. Luther humbly says that perhaps he "just became a habit."

Naturally, changes take place as time passes. You and your audience evolve, but your target demographic stays the same. Broadcasters have to work harder to retain their target audience and stay relevant, but Luther and I have learned how to maintain a balance. As roles shift and change, minor conflicts arise as we work together to carry on the tradition of WDEF Radio. Conflicts occasionally develop as competition grows, as other stations try unsuccessfully to imitate Sunny 92.3 and duplicate the history of WDEF Radio. That is not possible because Luther has stood the test of time; the history and tradition of WDEF Radio would not exist without him. When the natural conflicts of age difference and broadcasting content arise, we both understand that "work is work." When we experience disagreements, we know it is just part of the business. If we've had a bad day, later that evening I'll get a phone call from Luther asking me if I'm watching the History Channel. "Turn it on, quick," he'll say. "You've got to see this." The conflict is over. He never allows the tensions of the morning to carry over. That is the radio business. I am honored to work alongside Luther every day and face those challenges and to continue to carry on the long tradition of WDEF Radio.

Photo by Daisy Moffatt

Luther and James on the air at the WDEF studios, September 2012.

Photo by Daisy Moffatt

Luther and James share a laugh on the air at the WDEF studios,
September 2012.

Photo by Daisy Moffatt

Luther, James and Gene Lovin in the Sunny 92.3 WDEF studios,
September 2012.

Luther has received many offers from other markets over the years from places like Houston, Los Angeles, Philadelphia, Boston, and New York. Radio stations in these larger markets would read about Luther in industry periodicals and newspapers. Seeing his consistently high ratings, they would contact him. According to Luther, these radio executives would have meetings and decide, "Let's hire him and see how well he can do out here." But Luther never accepted. He even received an offer from media mogul Ted Turner, but Luther loved where he was and what he was doing. He loved Chattanooga.

I've received many offers over the years. "Let's hire this country boy from Tennessee and see what he can do for the ratings," they'd say. So they'd make me an offer, but I love this town. That's the reason I did not go, plus they did not have Nehi Grape {laughs}. Like I've said before, my father died and I had my mother to take care of, as well as a younger brother and sister. I just wasn't interested. I loved my town and I wanted to stay here and that is what I did.

Ted Turner once made me an offer as well. He had one of the stations here in town that he owned and had sold and wanted me to come down to Atlanta. So I went down and had an interview. He said, "I'll tell you what I'll do, Luther. I'll give you everything that the company has put into your retirement plan. Whatever it is, I'll give it to you, plus some more. I'll give you a nice raise if you will come to work for me." I said, "Mr. Turner, I appreciate this, and I've read a lot about you. I know you're a McCallie graduate and I read a lot about you while you were in school. I admire you very much and respect what you are trying to do in the broadcasting field, but I just don't feel like I should leave my company, WDEF, at this time." He responded by saying, "Well, if you change your mind, you give me a call."

Luther never did change his mind and has remained faithful to WDEF and to Chattanooga for the entirety of his ongoing career. I asked Luther's daughter Joanie what she wanted her dad to be remembered for, specifically in terms of his identity. "Things have changed so much; things are different. When I was growing up, you listened to Dad and that is how you got all of your information. Everything that you needed to know about anything that was going on, you listened to Dad. Things have changed. People get their information differently now, but I guess he hasn't changed. He has stayed the same and his values have always remained the same. His commitment to people and to Chattanooga has always remained the same. Being away from Chattanooga for so long, I want people to remember him for that commitment and for his love for the city. I want people to remember the fact that he has been in Chattanooga for so long. I want him to be remembered for that and for what he has done for the city of Chattanooga."

I am certain the people of Chattanooga will always remember Luther and the impact he has had on the city. He has had an amazing career and, during an interview, spoke about what matters to him most at this point in his job:

At this stage of my life, it's nice to be received for the work that you do. The reception you receive from people that you meet out in the public just tickles you. They look at you and, in most cases, admire you and that just tickles you down to your gizzard {laughs}. The main thing is the job and making a success of that. It's that kind of thing that is a great reward in this business.

Luther is often recognized after being in this business for many decades. Even when I first started at WDEF more than 20 years ago, people everywhere recognized Luther because he had been on WDEF Radio and Television from the beginning. Luther truly is as he has been described, a "Chattanooga tradition." Luther's wife Mary says, "I am just so grateful to the people of Chattanooga that they have accepted him as a friend. Whenever we go somewhere, anyone that speaks to Luther or recognizes him does so with such admiration, with such a feeling of friendship. They feel that way because it is true; he is their friend. He has given his whole life to this town through his voice and through the promotion of this town, *his* town. He is proud of Chattanooga and he always has been. He has always loved Chattanooga, and the people here have been so good to him. His sponsors have stuck with him and have been great, and most of all, we appreciate the love that the people of Chattanooga have shown him."

Luther's family and the people of Chattanooga have one more reason to be proud of a man that has dedicated his life to them and to the broadcasting industry. In November 2012, with a career that is unmatched by any other broadcaster in history, Luther Masingill was inducted into the National Radio Hall of Fame. After more than 70 years of being on the same station in the same time slot, Luther received the ultimate accolade in the radio industry. The National Radio Hall of Fame Chairman Bruce DuMont said, "Luther Masingill has played an important role in American radio history. He is a warm, personable, talented performer and communicator who chose to stay in one market – Chattanooga, Tennessee – for his entire career. Luther decided not to follow the traditional zigzag road to the top of what could have been a very lucrative career. But Luther loved Chattanooga, where he found his niche, and worked his way into the heart and soul of a city, his state and his country. His fans from several generations have benefited from Luther's decision." Our very own Luther became a member of the National Radio Hall of Fame on November 10, 2012, in Chicago, Illinois. Prior to the induction ceremony, here is what Luther had to say on receiving such a high honor:

Receiving this award is an honor. I'm really flattered. I never thought I would get it. There are people more important in the radio business than I am. I have been on a small station here, small compared to a lot of them, but I am flattered. I want to know if they have been talking to my doctor? Has he told them something he hasn't told me? {Laughs} No, I am just joking, but I would like to continue what I'm doing and take my number of years left right here where I am sitting now, in the studio with the morning show crew, with you and Kim and Gene. There are no plans for anything else. I don't think they could talk me into it. But yes, I am flattered that they would consider me for that honor.

According to the National Radio Hall of Fame, Luther was inducted along with Terry Gross of National Public Radio, Jack L. Cooper, radio's first African-American disc jockey, Ron Chapman, Dallas radio icon, Art Laboe, oldies pioneer and syndicated radio personality from Los Angeles, Gary Burbank, legendary WLW/Cincinnati broadcaster, and Howard Stern, one of radio's "true game changers." Prior to the ceremony, I asked Luther what he thought about being inducted in the same class along with Howard Stern.

Are they going to seat me beside Mr. Stern? I wonder what he's going to say to me? "You ugly little Southern boy." You don't think he's going to do that do you? {Laughs} I'm looking forward to meeting him. I've heard a lot about him. Remember this about human beings: there's always good in everybody. I am sure there's some good in him, and I'll try to bring it out without him hitting me too hard. As for being inducted into the National Radio Hall of Fame, it's gratifying after all these years. It's something you've tried to do your best at the whole time you are doing it, and it is a compliment when someone bestows an honor on you. This is a great honor. I do appreciate it. Oh, and please spell my last name right! {Laughs}

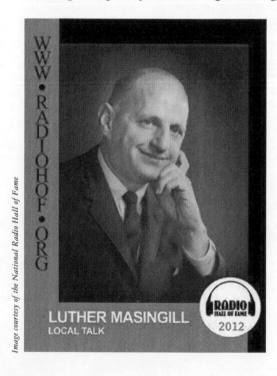

This image of Luther now hangs in the National Radio Hall of Fame & Museum in Chicago, November 2012.

Luther is inducted into the National Radio Hall of Fame, November 2012.

Luther and Mary at the National Radio Hall of Fame induction ceremony,
November 2012.

Photo by David Carroll

Luther shares a laugh with Geraldo Rivera, the host of the National Radio Hall of Fame induction ceremony, November 2012.

Photo by David Carroll

Geraldo Rivera, Luther and Ralph Emery at the National Radio Hall of Fame induction ceremony, November 2012.

Luther has had an amazing journey. Long before I was born, Luther was already walking down the road toward broadcasting greatness. In my small world as a child, all I knew is that he found my dog Andy and healed the broken heart of a little boy. Now, I work alongside my childhood hero every day. I had the distinct honor of being with him the night he was inducted into the National Radio Hall of Fame.

I have watched him help countless others find pets they love and things they've lost. I've watched him help people in whatever way he can and serve as an ambassador for the city of Chattanooga. I have listened to Luther go from my breakfast table in the morning, to the breakfast table of the next generation. He has given his life to broadcasting and to the city of Chattanooga. He has become a broadcasting legend with hard work, commitment, and one simple philosophy, a consistent attempt to help his fellow man.

*I guess I'd put it like this: my philosophy on life, in one word, would be **love**, and you're using that in all kinds of different ways. There's the love for Jesus Christ, the love for your family, the love for your children, the love that you display to other people. Yes, **love**, in one word, to describe life. If you've got it, if you receive it, you've got it made. It's like amaretto pie from the Mt. Vernon Restaurant {laughs}.*

I believe Luther will leave a legacy of love and compassion to his family, friends, and to the city of Chattanooga. He has left his mark in this world with an unprecedented career and has done it with basic philosophies that we can all aspire to achieve, regardless of our chosen profession. In Luther's case, it was broadcasting, achieved through one simple philosophy: helping others. In this glimpse into the life of a truly legendary broadcaster and human being, a tribute to a life well lived, I hope you were able to find a little bit of yourself in the recounting of my own life with Luther. I will continue my journey alongside him, and when it's our time, Luther and I will go into the studio and we'll go live on the air. The red light above the studio entrance will be on. Only this time, I'll be on the other side of the studio glass, working alongside my childhood hero and the most familiar name and voice in Chattanooga, Luther Masingill, otherwise known as…Luther.

Photo by Daisy Moffatt

Acknowledgements

To our spouses and children. You have proven to be patient and long-suffering as this project has taken almost three years to complete. After working on it in between life's demands, we knew there was no better time than the present to complete it. We couldn't have done it without you. Thank you, Christy, Gracie, and Lucy. Thank you, Matt, Shannon, and Iain.

Luther and Mary Masingill. Thank you for your gracious cooperation during the information-gathering portion of this book and for granting us access to the photos that have chronicled your lives. It is an honor to have spent this time with you and to share your story and broadcasting history with the world.

Jeffrey Masingill and Joanie Masingill Brown. Thank you for opening up your hearts to us and for sharing your memories and experiences. Because of you, the world has a clearer picture of who your dad really is, both personally and professionally.

Doris Ellis. Thank you for opening up and sharing the WDEF-TV Archives with us and for graciously imparting your extensive knowledge and expertise while we reviewed the materials for our publication. Your kindness and assistance proved invaluable, and this project would not have been the same without you.

Phillip W. Rodgers and Bees with Flashlights Publishing Company. Thank you for always making yourself available for consulting and advice during this project. Your experience and extensive knowledge of the publishing industry proved invaluable.

Daisy and Beau Moffatt of Daisy Moffatt Photography. Thank you for the in-studio photographs and back cover photo. The care and professionalism you bring to a project is invaluable. You are truly at the top of your class among professional photographers.

Kim Wheeler. Thank you for your careful and meticulous critique during the editing of this project. This story conveyed to the reader is a better one thanks to your critical eye and expertise.

Danny Howard. Thank you for teaching and mentoring us over the years. Your knowledge in the business of radio broadcasting is second to none.

To the staff, both past and present, at WDEF and WDOD Radio. You are like a second family. We share the understanding that we have all, at one time or another, had the honor of working alongside Luther, one of the most amazing men in broadcasting history.

About the Authors

James D. Howard has been a radio personality for WDEF Sunny 92.3 since 1993 and has been working by Luther's side on the morning show since 2001. He has been a Chattanooga resident all of his life and cannot remember a time when he did not listen to Luther in the morning. James has a true heart for our military men and women and since 2004 has made goodwill mission trips to Iraq, Afghanistan and Kuwait, traveling during the Christmas holidays to visit troops from the Chattanooga area. He has authored two children's books, donating all proceeds to T.C. Thompson Children's Hospital and the Epilepsy Foundation of Southeast Tennessee. He is also a commercial-rated pilot who flies in the Coast Guard Auxiliary. His most recent venture is the creation of the non-profit organization called Aviation Smiley Face, where local teachers are provided with flight lessons to encourage them to communicate to their students the importance of the math and science skills learned through aviation. James resides in Chattanooga, Tennessee, with his wife, Christy, his two daughters, Gracie and Lucy, and his dogs, Wilson and Lily.

Holly Abernathy is a published writer and photographer. She got her start in broadcast communications at WDEF Radio as an intern in college, gaining experience in all aspects of the industry. Upon graduation, she was hired as a full-time employee at Sunny 92.3 WDEF Radio. She did overnights, gaining on-air experience as well. She left WDEF as promotions director in 2007 after the birth of her daughter. She continues to do freelance work, secondary to raising her children, who were both born in Chattanooga. You can find more on her website at 6qCreative.com. She lives in Nashville, Tennessee, with her husband and two children.

Made in the USA
Lexington, KY
18 August 2013